South Carolina's Wetlands

Status and Trends, 1982 – 1989

T. E. Dahl
U.S. Fish and Wildlife Service
Division of Habitat Conservation
Habitat Assessment Branch

Acknowledgments

This study was funded in part by the Environmental Protection Agency (EPA), Office of Wetlands, Oceans and Watersheds under interagency agreement number DW149356-01-0. Special appreciation is due to Doreen Vetter and Chris Williams of the EPA, Wetlands Division, Washington, D.C.

The author would like to recognize the extraordinary efforts of two people of the Wetlands Status and Trends Unit of the U.S. Fish and Wildlife Service. Mr. Richard Young was responsible for the integrity and geographic information system analysis of the data. Ms. Martha Caldwell assisted in the field work and conducted the statistical analysis of the data sets.

Many other people on the staff at the National Wetlands Inventory Center of the U.S. Fish and Wildlife Service in St. Petersburg, FL contributed to this effort. Their help is greatly appreciated.

Dr. Kenneth Burnham of Colorado State University, Fort Collins, CO wrote the statistical analysis programs.

Publication design and layout was done by the U.S. Geological Survey, Madison, WI.

This report should be cited as follows: Dahl, T.E. 1999. South Carolina's wetlands — status and trends 1982 – 1989. U.S. Department of the Interior, Fish and Wildlife Service, Washington, D.C. 58 pp.

Front cover photo: Estuarine emergents, Edisto River, South Carolina
T. Dahl

Back cover photo: White water-lily (Nymphaea odorata)
USFWS

United States Department of the Interior
Fish and Wildlife Service

United States Environmental Protection Agency

Conversion Table

U S Customary to Metric

inches (in)	x	25 40	=	millimeters (mm)
inches (in)	x	2 54	=	centimeters (cm)
feet (ft)	x	0 3048	=	meters (m)
miles (mi)	x	1 609	=	kilometers (km)
nautical miles (nmi)	x	1 852	=	kilometers (km)
square feet (ft^2)	x	0 0929	=	square meters (m^2)
square miles (mi^2)	x	2 590	=	square kilometers (km^2)
acres (A)	x	0 4047	=	hectares (ha)
gallons (gal)	x	3 785	=	liters (L)
cubic feet (ft^3)	x	0 02831	=	cubic meters (m^3)
acre-feet (A-ft)	x	1233 5	=	cubic meters (m^3)
ounces (oz)	x	28 3495	=	grams (g)
pounds (lb)	x	0 4536	=	kilograms (kg)
short tons (tons)	x	0 9072	=	metric tons (t)
British Thermal Units (BTU)	x	0 2520	=	kilocalories (kcal)
Farenheit degrees (F)		0 5556 (F - 32)	=	Celsius degrees (C)

Metric to U S Customary

millimeters (mm)	x	0 03937	=	inches (in)
centimeters (cm)	x	0 3937	=	inches (in)
meters (m)	x	3 281	=	feet (ft)
kilometers (km)	x	0 6214	=	miles (mi)
square meters (m^2)	x	10 764	=	square feet (ft^2)
square kilometers (km^2)	x	0 3861	=	square miles (mi^2)
hectares (ha)	x	2 471	=	acres (A)
liters (L)	x	0 2642	=	gallons (gal)
cubic meters (m^3)	x	35 31	=	cubic feet (ft^3)
cubic meters (m^3)	x	0 0008110	=	acre-feet (A-ft)
milligrams (mg)	x	0 00003527	=	ounces (oz)
grams (g)	x	0 03527	=	ounces (oz)
kilograms (kg)	x	2 2046	=	ounces (oz)
metric tons (t)	x	2204 62	=	pounds (lb)
metric tons (t)	x	1 102	=	short tons (tons)
kilocalories (kcal)	x	3 968	=	British Thermal Units (BTU)
Celsius degrees (C)		1 8(C) + 32	=	Farenheit degrees (F)

Contents

Executive Summary 7

Introduction 8

Historical Background 9

Study Area 14

Estimating South Carolina's Wetland Resources 19

South Carolina's Wetlands — Common Community Associations 21

Results: Status, Distribution and Ownership of Wetlands 30

Wetland Trends, 1982–89 40

Discussion of Wetland Trends 44

Summary 49

References Cited 50

Appendix A: Definitions of Habitat Categories Used in the
South Carolina Status and Trends Study 53

Appendix B: Data Table 57

Appendix C: Data Table — Combined categories 58

List of Figures

Figure 1. Estimated extent of South Carolina's original wetlands 9

Figure 2. Regions of historical commercial rice producing wetlands in South Carolina 9

Figure 3. A 1989 high altitude infrared photograph shows patterns of old rice fields and levees
along the Ashepoo River, Colleton County, South Carolina 10

Figure 4. An infrared photograph of primarily forested wetland along the Pee Dee River, South Carolina, 1990 11

Figure 5. Location and construction date of the major reservoirs in South Carolina 12

Figure 6. A 1990 aerial infrared photograph of "Carver's Bay", Georgetown County, South Carolina 13

Figure 7. The four physiographic zones within South Carolina used in this study 14

Figure 8. Three major segments of South Carolina's coast 15

Figure 9. The South Carolina portion of the Coastal Barrier Resources System 16

Figure 10. Major rivers and (watershed) basins within South Carolina. 17

Figure 11. South Carolina counties 18

Figure 12. Major land use categories within South Carolina 18

Figure 13. Randomized sample plot distribution for this study. 19

Figure 14a-d. Wetland area (a) as compared to total area of the State; (b) percent by estuarine and
freshwater types; (c) estuarine covertypes; (d) freshwater covertypes 30

Figure 15. Estuarine emergent wetlands along South Carolina's coast 31

Figure 16. Estuarine wetland distribution along South Carolina's coast, 1989 32

Figure 17. Palustrine (freshwater) wetland distribution within South Carolina, 1989 33

Figure 18. Forested wetland distribution within South Carolina, 1989 37

Figure 19. Graphic representation of wetland resource areas in South Carolina, 1989 37

Figure 20. Change in wetlands (as a percentage) converted to various land uses in South Carolina
between 1982 and 1989 40

Figure 21. Conversion and loss of forested wetland in South Carolina, 1982-1989 41

Figure 22. An example of wetland loss to "other upland" land use in Horry County, South Carolina 42

Figure 23. An illustration of major Federal land units in South Carolina 43

Figure 24. Metropolitan lands in South Carolina and losses of wetland to upland urban development 43

Figure 25. Conversion from forested wetland to emergent wetland 45

Figure 26. Managed pine plantation of South Carolina's coastal plain 46

Figure 27. Population growth in South Carolina counties between 1980 and 1990 48

Figure 28. Wetland resource areas of South Carolina that may face future threat for conversion to upland land uses ...48

List of Tables

Table 1a–e. Wetland habitat descriptions, characteristic plant species and classification designation as found in this study.

    (a) Wetland types of South Carolina's Appalachian Highlands (Blue Ridge) 22

    (b) Wetland types of South Carolina's Gulf-Atlantic Rolling Plain (Piedmont) 23

    (c) Wetland types common to both South Carolina's Gulf-Atlantic Rolling Plain (Piedmont) and Coastal Flats ... 24

    (d) Wetland types of South Carolina's Coastal Flats 27

    (e) Wetland types of South Carolina's Coastal Zone. 29

Table 2. Distribution of all palustrine wetland types by physiographic region in South Carolina as found in this study, 1989 33

Table 3. Estimated acreage of wetlands by covertype classes within the physiographic regions of South Carolina, 1989 34

Table 4. Average area and size range of palustrine wetlands as they appeared within the sample units for South Carolina in 1989 36

Table 5. Area of reserves and publicly owned lands that may contain wetlands in South Carolina 38

Table 6. Estimated wetland area in South Carolina in 1982 and 1989 and the change(s) as reported for various categories in this study 41

Table 7. Potential timber and pulp production effects to wetlands 47

Executive Summary

This study examined 465 sample plots distributed throughout South Carolina. Aerial photographs were used in combination with field verification to determine changes in wetland area between 1982 and 1989.

The results indicate that South Carolina had an estimated 4,104,850 acres (1,661,880 ha) of wetlands in 1989; 89 percent were freshwater wetlands. Eleven percent were estuarine (saltwater) wetlands. Palustrine forested wetlands made up 70 percent of the total wetland area.

The average annual net loss of wetlands observed during this study was 2,920 acres (1,182 ha). Total wetland area declined by 0.5 percent from 1982 to 1989. Palustrine forested wetlands suffered the biggest losses, declining 5.1 percent, while palustrine shrub wetlands realized the largest gains, increasing by 33.4 percent. The rate of wetland loss in South Carolina had declined by 48 percent compared to previously reported results.

Loss of estuarine wetlands was minimal. Estuarine wetlands declined by 109 acres (44 ha), making the average annual loss of estuarine wetlands statistically insignificant.

Collectively agriculture, forestry and urbanization were responsible for 81 percent of all the observed freshwater wetland losses between 1982 and 1989. Forestry accounted for 31 percent of the losses, agriculture (exclusive of farmed wetland conversions) was responsible for 28 percent and urban expansion 22 percent, respectively.

Agricultural conversion of wetlands was evenly split between the Coastal Flats and the Rolling Plain (Piedmont). Conversion of wetlands to silvicultural land use was primarily restricted to the Coastal Flats portion of the state. An estimated 55 percent of all palustrine wetlands were found on or adjacent to agricultural lands. Urban expansion converted wetlands in various locations. Most notable occurrences were observed in the Hilton Head area, Charleston and North Charleston and in the vicinity of Myrtle Beach and Columbia. The impacts of rural development on wetland losses were most notable in Horry County.

From 1982 to 1989, forested wetlands diminished in area by 155,500 acres (62,960 ha). Of the forested wetlands where the trees were removed, most remained as some other type of wetland. Of the forested wetlands lost to upland land uses, an estimated 40 percent or 5,340 acres (2,160 ha) were lost to upland managed pine plantations.

When all wetland losses and gains were tallied, South Carolina had not attained no-net-loss of wetland area within the time frame of the study.

South Carolina estuarine intertidal wetland
T. Dahl

Introduction

The U.S. Fish and Wildlife Service (Service) has major responsibility for the protection and stewardship of migratory and endangered fish and wildlife and their habitats. The agency is concerned with changes in the status of wetlands as they potentially affect any migratory and endangered species. The Service has undertaken wetlands inventory and monitoring activities in the past resulting in the production of wetland maps, reports and trends studies.

This study was conducted to provide recent information on the extent and trends of South Carolina's wetlands.

South Carolina occupies a key position in the Southeastern Coastal Plain and, like many states, faces accelerating demands on its natural resources.

This report presents the results of a study of wetland changes in South Carolina between 1982 and 1989. It provides estimates of the status of wetland area within the State, and losses or gains that occurred during the study time frame. The trends data have been supplemented with additional sources of information on wetland ownership and community types to provide the reader with a more complete picture of South Carolina's wetland resources.

Freshwater wetlands near Elloree, South Carolina
T. Dahl

Historical Background

From soil records and historical maps it is possible to estimate the past extent of South Carolina's wetlands. Although precise information is not available on the area and type of wetlands, some estimates indicate that as much as 32 percent of the State's area, up to 6.4 million acres (2.6 million ha), were wetland during the 1700s (Dahl 1990). Coastal marshes, riverine swamps, isolated bays and pocosins made up the majority of the wetland habitats (Figure 1).

Beginning with native North American habitation of the area now known South Carolina, human use and occupation has modified the landscape and had an impact on the number and type of wetlands. In South Carolina, the coastal region or "low country" was the first area to attract European settlements (Garrett 1988). Early settlers followed the river systems to the interior using them as a means of transportation. Traditional small farms and subsistence agriculture were replaced by plantations during the colonial period and wetland drainage and modification became prevalent. As early as 1754, South Carolina authorized drainage of the Cacaw Swamp for agricultural use (Beauchamp 1987).

Plantation owners did not always seek to drain wetlands. In the coastal regions some plantation owners found that the immense coastal marshlands supported by major rivers were capable of being irrigated with every flood tide by fresh water and vast areas of marshlands were diked and the water regulated to support rice growing operations (Lucas 1980). As early as the 1670s rice formed one of South Carolina's commercially valuable commodities (Salley 1919) and by the 1850s South Carolina was the largest producer of rice in the United States and its territories, with an estimated yield of about 160 million pounds (72 million kg) statewide (Littlefield 1995). Tidal rice culture was practiced along the Savannah, Combahee, Ashpoo, Edisto and Cooper rivers, but the largest historical rice growing area was located in the lower reaches of the Santee, Sampit, Black, Pee Dee and Waccamaw River deltas. Major historical rice growing areas of South Carolina are shown in Figure 2. Today, many of South Carolina's historic rice fields remain

Figure 1. Estimated extent of South Carolina's original wetlands. Adapted from historic map information and extrapolation of hydric soils from the State Soil Survey Geographic Data Base.

Figure 2. Regions of historical commercial rice producing wetlands in South Carolina (Sources: Kovacik and Winberry 1987; Littlefield 1995).

as wetland (Figure 3). Commercial rice growing operations have declined, leaving these areas to revert to tidal marshlands.

Throughout the State's history, river systems have been active forces helping to shape the physical geography and influence cultural land uses. Both the use and conservation of many of the State's natural resources stem from the wealth of these rivers. Historically, South Carolina contained at least 20 large rivers that flowed unimpeded from the interior to the Atlantic Ocean. These rivers nourished the coastal marshes and were bordered by broad expanses of alluvial low lands, forested swamps or bottomlands supporting many water tolerant hardwood tree species (Figure 4). In some regions of the coastal plain these bottomland wetlands were from two to six miles (9.7 km) wide (Lucas 1980) and represented a tremendous source of commercial forest resources.

The cypress trees *(Taxodium distichum)* that were characteristic of many of these bottomland swamps were an important source of timber for pioneering settlers (Ewel and Odum 1984). During the 1800s baldcypress became a highly prized commercial forest product because of its durability and resistance to termites and rotting under humid conditions (Williams 1989). Cypress trees were exploited extensively throughout the 1800s and the first half of this century. By the 1850s there were 50 sawmills operating around Aiken, South Carolina near the headwaters of the Savannah and Edisto rivers. By the 1950s standing baldcypress stands had been greatly reduced.

Although cypress logs were used extensively during the 1800s, some of the wettest hardwood areas went untouched. While logging of the hardwood species

Figure 3. A 1989 high altitude infrared photograph shows patterns of old rice fields and levees (mottled blue) along the Ashepoo River, Colleton County, South Carolina.

began in the swamps of South Carolina sometime prior to 1900 (Durham 1967), the deep swamps of the Great Pee Dee and Santee rivers were considered too inaccessible for timber harvesting until sometime following 1900. It is estimated that South Carolina's first growth timber harvest peaked around the mid-1920s (Williams 1989). Following this period, most of the swamp forests in South Carolina had been logged at least once.

Forested wetlands in the southeastern United States are highly productive ecosystems because of periodic inputs of floodwater, sediment and nutrients (Taylor *et al.* 1990). Within the wet bottomland forests there occur variations in canopy type and height based on responses of plant species tolerance to soil inundation from the wettest to the driest. Usually these communities support populations of mammals, amphibians and crawfish (Wharton *et al.* 1981). The Congaree Swamp in South Carolina supports the second highest density of birds (1634 birds/sq km) of the eastern deciduous forests (Winton 1980). Taylor *et al.* (1990) described the functions and values of bottomland hardwood forests in greater detail. Of the total area in South Carolina that was originally forested wetland, some has been drained and converted to upland silvicultural uses, some has been logged and re-planted or regenerated naturally, other areas have been cleared for agricultural production or urban development. Today the poorly drained soils that made up many of the original wetlands in the southeastern United States are some of the most intensively managed forest sites in the world (Allen and Campbell 1988).

South Carolina has 11,000 miles (17,699 km) of permanently flowing rivers and streams (Beasley *et al.* 1988). Reservoirs have been created on every major river

Figure 4. An infrared photograph of primarily forested wetland along the Pee Dee River, South Carolina, 1990. Historically, forested wetlands along riverine systems were extensive and provided a source of timber through the 1800s.

system in South Carolina with the exception of the Pee Dee. Although hundreds of small millpond impoundments were built within the State during the 18th and 19th centuries, the 20th century has seen the construction of large water retention dams. In some cases impounding the rivers drowned tracts of bottomland forested wetlands, in other instances wetland areas were created by flooding backwater pools and bays. The location and date of construction of some of the major reservoirs on South Carolina's rivers are shown in Figure 5.

One of the more unusual wetland types that have been impacted over time is the "Carolina bay". Carolina bays are oval or elliptical depressions of unknown origin (Sharitz and Gibbons 1982). These wet-lands were originally by-passed by settlers but eventually the rich soils enticed drainage and conversion to agriculture (Kovacik and Winberry 1987). It has been estimated that South Carolina originally contained about 4,000 Carolina bay wetlands of various sizes (Richardson and Gibbons 1993). There is no accurate accounting of the number of Carolina bays that have been converted to upland

uses or those that have been ditched or partially drained. Over the past 200 years many have been converted to agriculture or upland forestry and some estimates are that very few of the original number of bays in South Carolina remain undisturbed (Bebber 1988). Figure 6 shows an aerial view of a Carolina bay bisected by a road and affected by other types of development.

Despite these historical trends, South Carolina still maintains numerous riverine swamp forests, productive salt marshes and freshwater wetlands. Overall, South Carolina ranks fifth in the Nation in wetland acreage expressed as a percent of surface area. Forested wetlands make up an important resource contributing 6 percent of the National total forested wetland area and 9 percent of the area within the southeastern United Sates. Two virgin or nearly virgin stands of bottomland forested swamp remain in South Carolina: The Congaree Swamp National Monument and the Francis Beidler Forest. These are two very rare examples of uncut swamp hardwood forest stands remaining in the southeastern United States (Durham 1967).

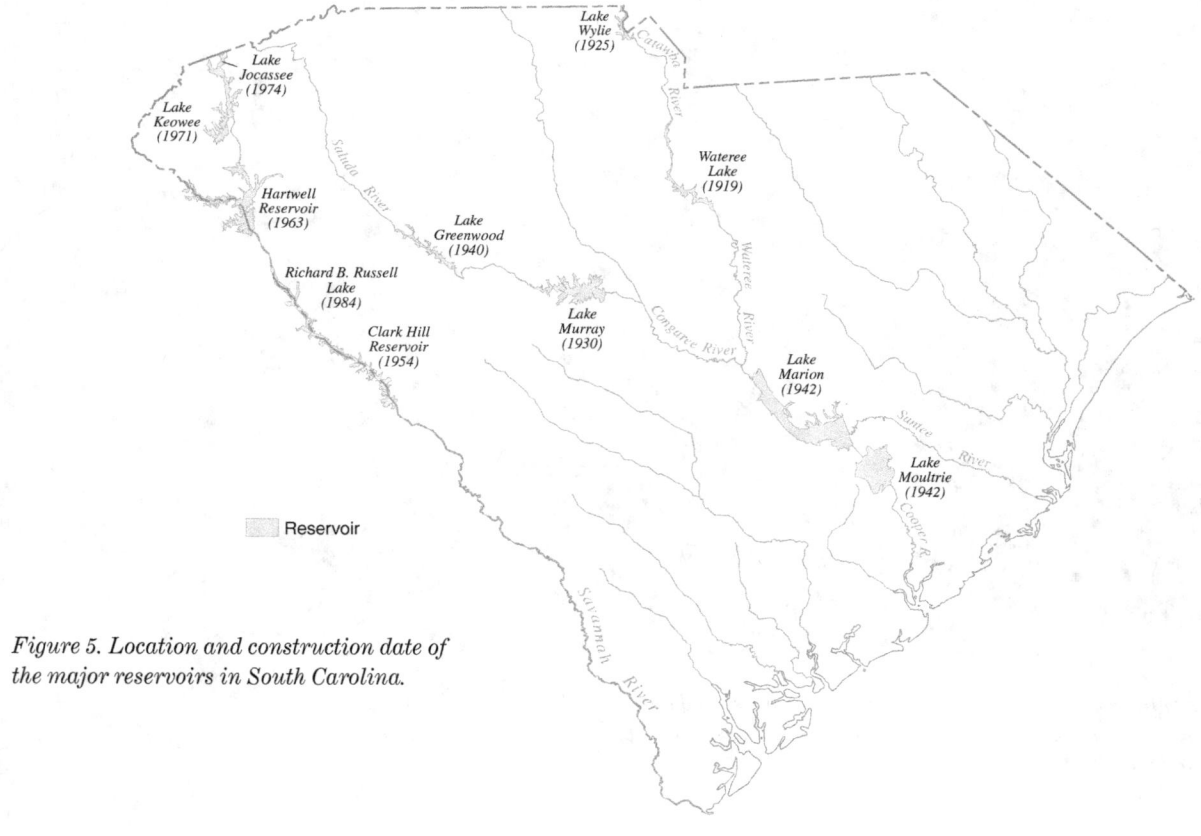

Figure 5. Location and construction date of the major reservoirs in South Carolina.

Figure 6. A 1990 aerial infrared photograph of "Carver's Bay", Georgetown County, South Carolina. This bay is bisected by a road and has been modified by encroaching land uses. In South Carolina all Carolina bays are oriented in a northwest/southeast direction.

Study Area

The total land area of South Carolina is approximately 19,320,552 acres (7,822,086 ha)[1]. The landscape varies in topographic relief from mountainous in the west to nearly level in the eastern portion of the Atlantic coastal plain.

For this study, South Carolina was stratified into four physiographic regions (Figure 7). These regions are described below.

Coastal Zone

Although not typically described by geographers as a unique region, a Coastal Zone region was considered in this study. The Coastal Zone encompasses the near-shore areas of the coast and includes barrier islands, coastal marshes, exposed tidal flats and other features not included in the landward physiographic zones. The Coastal Zone as described here is not synonymous with any state or Federal jurisdictional coastal zone definitions. It is an area where saltwater is the overriding influence on biological systems.

Within the Coastal Zone, South Carolina has 2,876 miles (4,628 km) of shore bordering the Atlantic Ocean. There are three distinct segments of the shore based on the geomorphic processes that formed each. These are shown in Figure 8 and include: The Grand Strand, a 100,000 year old barrier sand formation that extends from the North Carolina border south to Winyah Bay; the Santee Delta which is the largest deltaic complex on the east coast and; the Sea Island Complex composed of erosion remnant islands (that were part of the mainland at one time) and active barrier islands built by wind or wave action (South Carolina Coastal Council 1982). Included as part of this coastline are 198 miles (319 km) of recreational beaches and 153 miles (246 km) of barrier islands (Wells and Peterson n.d.).

Some segments of South Carolina's barrier islands have been designated as part of the Coastal Barrier Resources System. The Barrier Islands Act of 1983 removed undeveloped islands from Federal flood insurance protection and resulted in 13 locations along South Carolina's coastline being designated as coastal barriers under this legislation. The system was expanded to include several more sites by the Coastal Barrier Improvement Act. In all, 16 coastal barriers are part of the South Carolina System as shown in Figure 9.

---

[1] This study incorporated some estuarine embayments not included in the total land area figure.

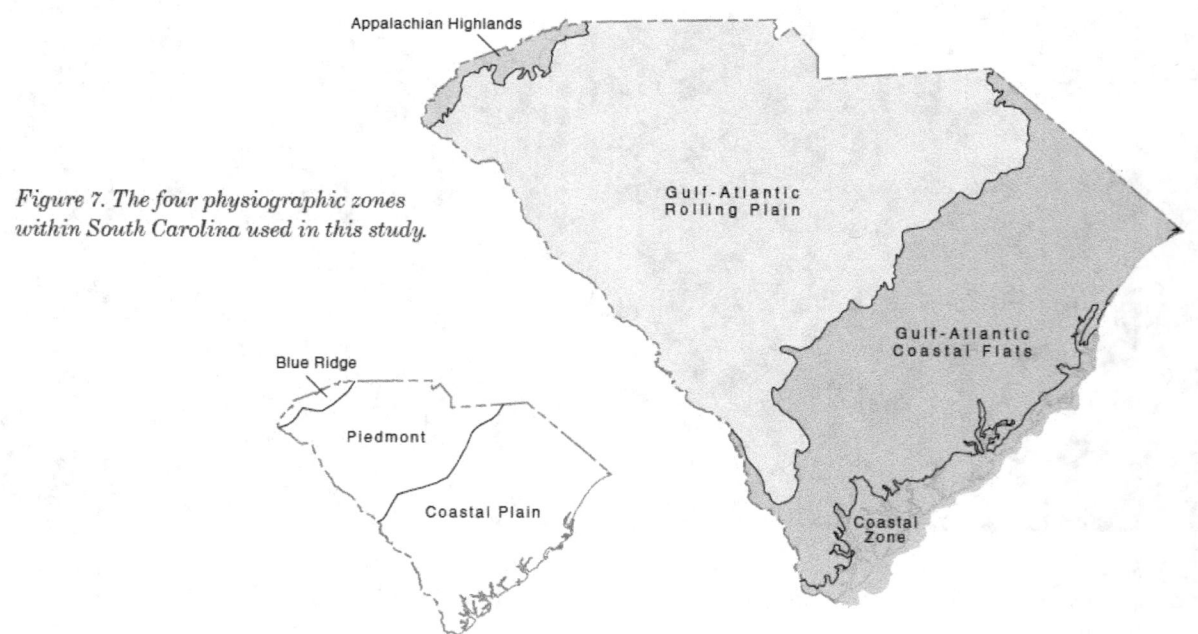

Figure 7. The four physiographic zones within South Carolina used in this study.

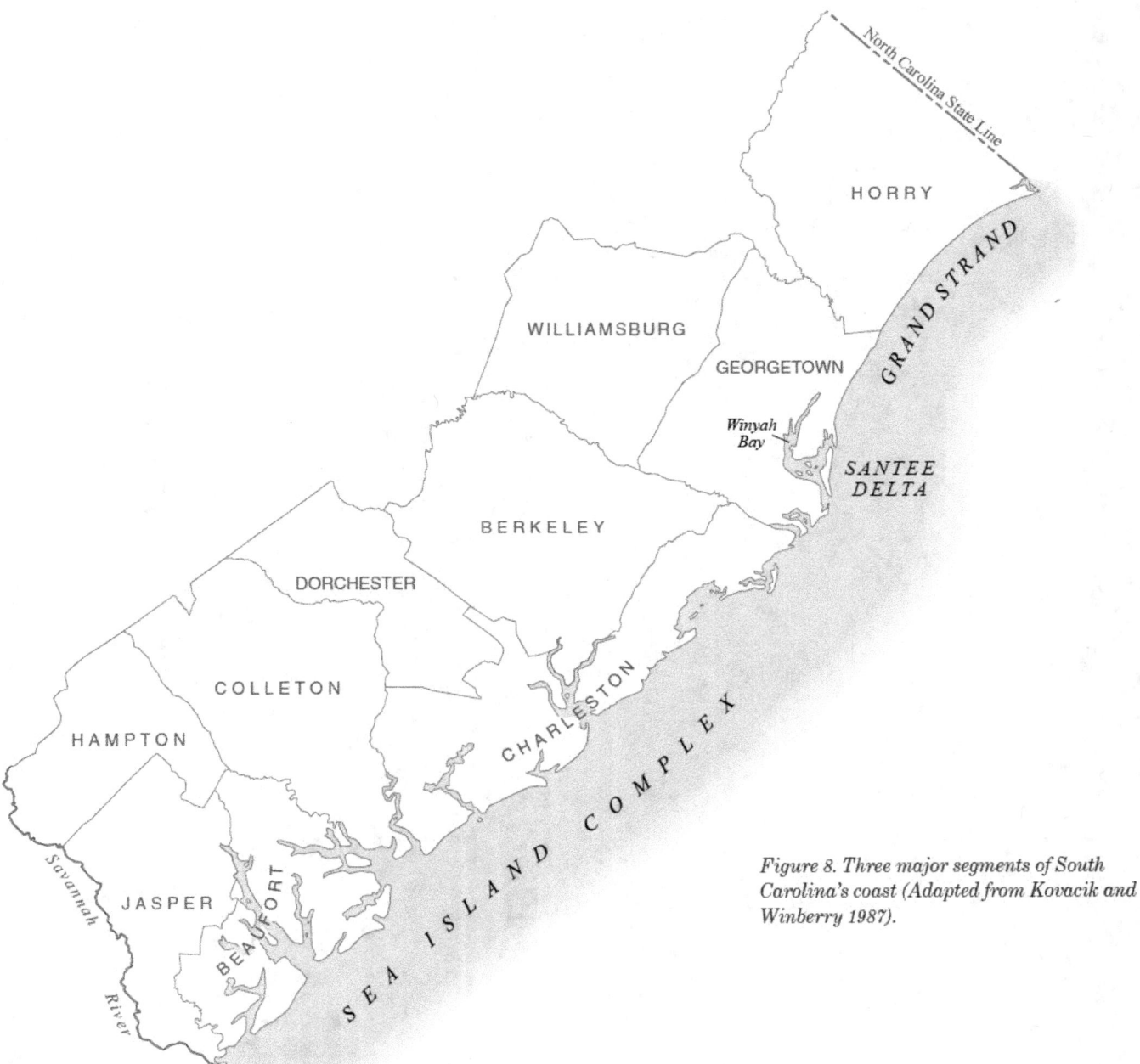

North Carolina State Line

HORRY

WILLIAMSBURG

GEORGETOWN

GRAND STRAND

Winyah
Bay

SANTEE
DELTA

BERKELEY

DORCHESTER

CHARLESTON

COLLETON

HAMPTON

SEA ISLAND COMPLEX

Savannah
River

JASPER

BEAUFORT

Figure 8. Three major segments of South
Carolina's coast (Adapted from Kovacik and
Winberry 1987).

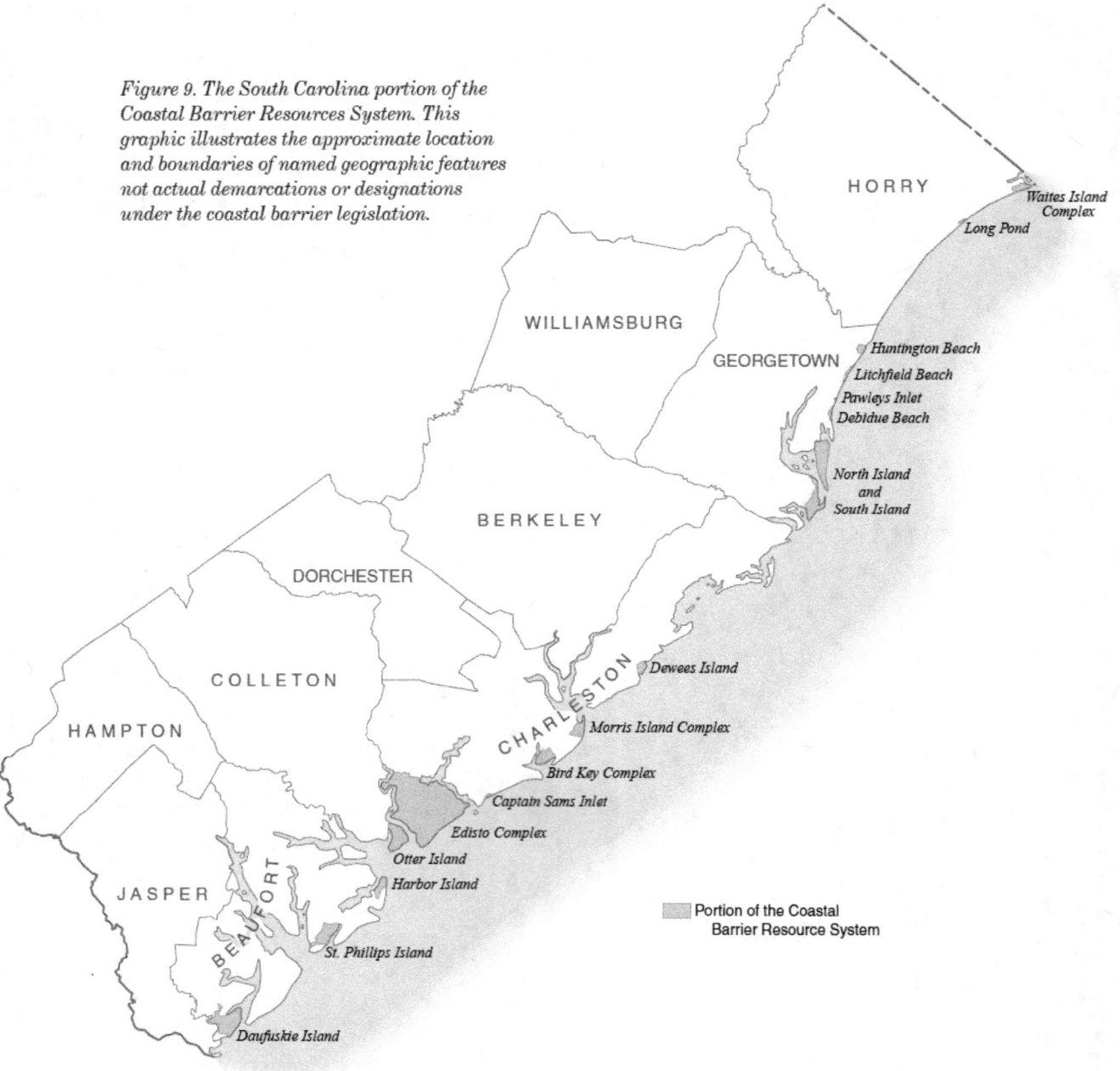

Figure 9. The South Carolina portion of the Coastal Barrier Resources System. This graphic illustrates the approximate location and boundaries of named geographic features not actual demarcations or designations under the coastal barrier legislation.

HORRY

WILLIAMSBURG

GEORGETOWN

BERKELEY

DORCHESTER

COLLETON

CHARLESTON

HAMPTON

JASPER

BEAUFORT

Waites Island Complex

Long Pond

Huntington Beach

Litchfield Beach

Pawleys Inlet

Debidue Beach

North Island and South Island

Dewees Island

Morris Island Complex

Bird Key Complex

Captain Sams Inlet

Edisto Complex

Otter Island

Harbor Island

St. Phillips Island

Daufuskie Island

Portion of the Coastal Barrier Resource System

Gulf-Atlantic Coastal Flats

The Gulf-Atlantic Coastal Flats developed from continental submergence and emergence with both erosion and deposition of soils (Colquhoun 1974). Soils originated either from the Appalachians or from coastal processes (McKnight *et al.* 1981) and they are composed of water borne deposits of sands, silt or clay and calcareous sediments. The Coastal Flats are characteristically level but small relief features affect drainage patterns and duration of inundation (Clark and Benforado 1981). Elevation on the Coastal Flats ranges from sea level to 300 feet (91 m). An unusual feature of the Coastal Flats in South Carolina is the occurrence of Carolina bays. These are oval or elliptical depressions that range in size from 4–5 acres (1.6–2.0 ha) to thousands of acres such as the bay that is the Big Swamp in Manchester State Forest in Sumter County (Kovacik and Winberry 1987). In South Carolina almost all of these bays are oriented in a northwest-southeasterly direction and unless artificially drained, all are wetlands.

Gulf-Atlantic Rolling Plain

The Gulf-Atlantic Rolling Plain as described by Hammond (1970) is nearly the same as the Piedmont within South Carolina. Others have used this term to describe this physiographic region which makes up roughly one-third of South Carolina (Meador 1995; Gibson 1994). This region is characterized by hilly topography; elevations range from 300 to 1200 feet (91–366 m). The rivers in this part of the State are long, with more gently sloped, wide valleys and carry heavy sediment loads (Kovacik and Winberry 1987).

Appalachian Highlands

The Appalachian Highlands or Blue Ridge Mountains are in the extreme northwestern portion of the state. The Blue Ridge is a small portion of the Appalachian Mountain System. It is the area of greatest topographic relief in South Carolina where elevations range from 1400 to over 3500 feet (427 to 1067 m). Streams in this region are fast-flowing and entrenched within steep valleys.

Other Geographical Features

Other important facets of South Carolina's geography that put wetland distribution into context relate to the watersheds, reservoirs and river drainage characteristics. The State is divided into four major watershed basins; the Pee Dee River Basin drains approximately 9 percent of South Carolina's land area, the Santee River Basin drains about 41 percent of the state, the ACE (Ashley-Combahee-Edisto) River Basin drains 32 percent of the State and, the Savannah River Basin drains about 18 percent of South Carolina (Figure 10).

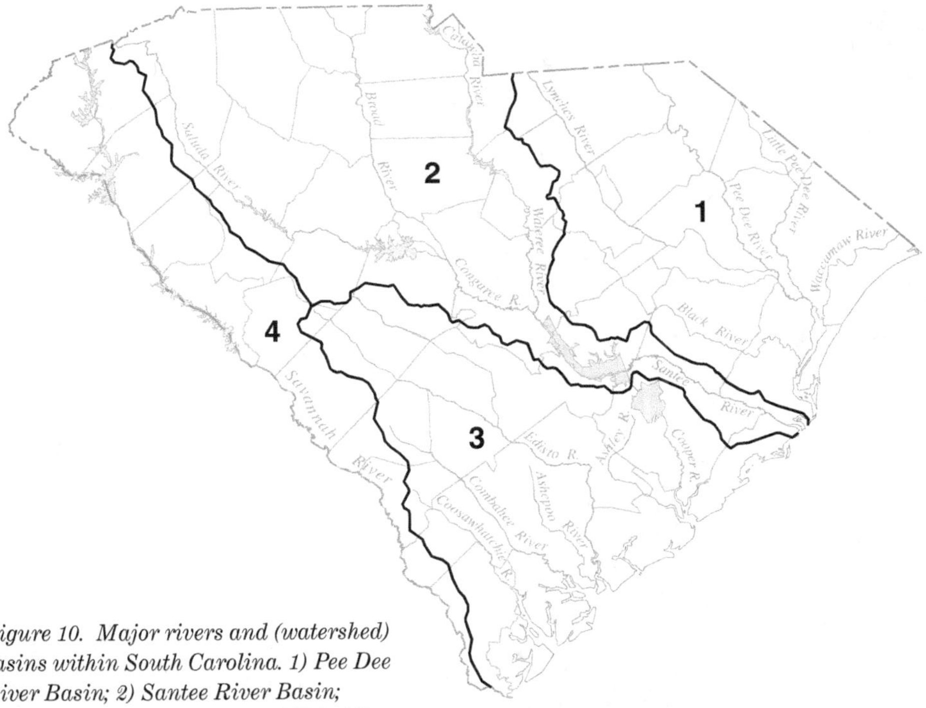

Figure 10. Major rivers and (watershed) basins within South Carolina. 1) Pee Dee River Basin; 2) Santee River Basin; 3) Ashley-Combahee-Edisto (ACE) River Basin; 4) Savannah River Basin (Source: Beasley et al. 1988).

Rivers draining the Rolling Plain (Piedmont) are typically colored yellow and red by silt and clay sediments. Rivers originating in the Coastal Flats typically meander and form wide, flat flood plains, channels or oxbows. They are often colored black from the high levels of tannic acid in the runoff from surrounding swamp hardwoods. The wetlands surrounding these rivers have thus acquired the colloquial terms of "red river bottoms" or "red river swamp" and "black water river bottoms" depending on the origins of the river waters. A further description of these and other terms used to describe wetland communities in South Carolina appear in Table 1a–e.

There are 46 counties in South Carolina (Figure 11). Major industries include tourism, agriculture, forestry and manufacturing. Orange-burg County is the leading agricultural county in South Carolina. It has the largest amount of land in farms in the State and ranks at or near the top of all counties for production of soybeans *(Glycine max.)*, corn *(Zea mays)*, wheat *(Triticum aestivum)*, cucumbers *(Cucumis sativus)*, watermelons *(Citrullus vulgaris)* and cantaloupes *(Cucumis melo)*, (De Francesco 1988). Land use in South Carolina is shown in Figure 12.

Figure 11. South Carolina counties.

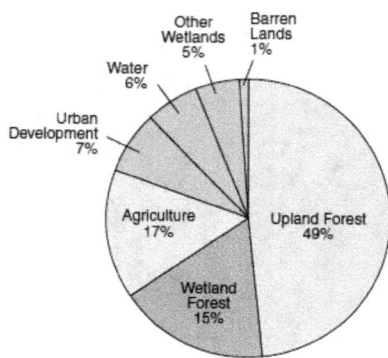

Figure 12. Major land use categories within South Carolina. Landuse categories are approximate based on the total area of the State as estimated by the Bureau of Census. This land area excludes some coastal embayments. Water area includes some vegetated wetlands and/or ponds as well as deepwater rivers and lakes (Source: South Carolina State Budget and Control Board 1994; Powell et al. 1993; U.S. Geological Survey 1970; this study).

Estimating South Carolina's Wetland Resources

Within the four physiographic strata described previously, sample plots (four square miles or 10.36 sq. km) were distributed at random. Four hundred sixty five sample plots were analyzed in this study (Figure 13). For each of these sample areas, aerial photography was acquired and stereoscopically interpreted to identify wetlands, deepwater habitats and uplands. Habitat category definitions are given in Appendix A.

The mean dates of the photography used to determine wetland trends in South Carolina were 1982 and 1989 with the difference being an average of 6.5 years. All photographs were color infrared and ranged from 1:58,000 to 1:40,000 scale. For this study, wetlands 3 acres (1.2 ha) and larger composed the target population[2]. Field verification of features on the aerial photography was done for approximately 10 percent of the sample. Rigorous quality control inspections were built into the interpretation, data collection and analysis processes. A more complete description of the techniques used to accomplish the interpretation, registration, and change detection is provided in various technical manuals (U.S. Fish and Wildlife Service 1994a, 1995; Dahl and Johnson 1991).

Changes in areal extent or type of wetland observed on the sample plots between 1983 and 1989 were recorded. Statistical estimates were used to expand the sample data to specific physiographic regions, wetland types or were generated for the entire State. The percent coefficient of variation associated with each estimate was also calculated.

[2] Actual results indicate that for each wetland catagory included in this study the minimum size represented was less than 1.0 acre (0.4 ha). However, not all wetlands less than the target size catagory were detected.

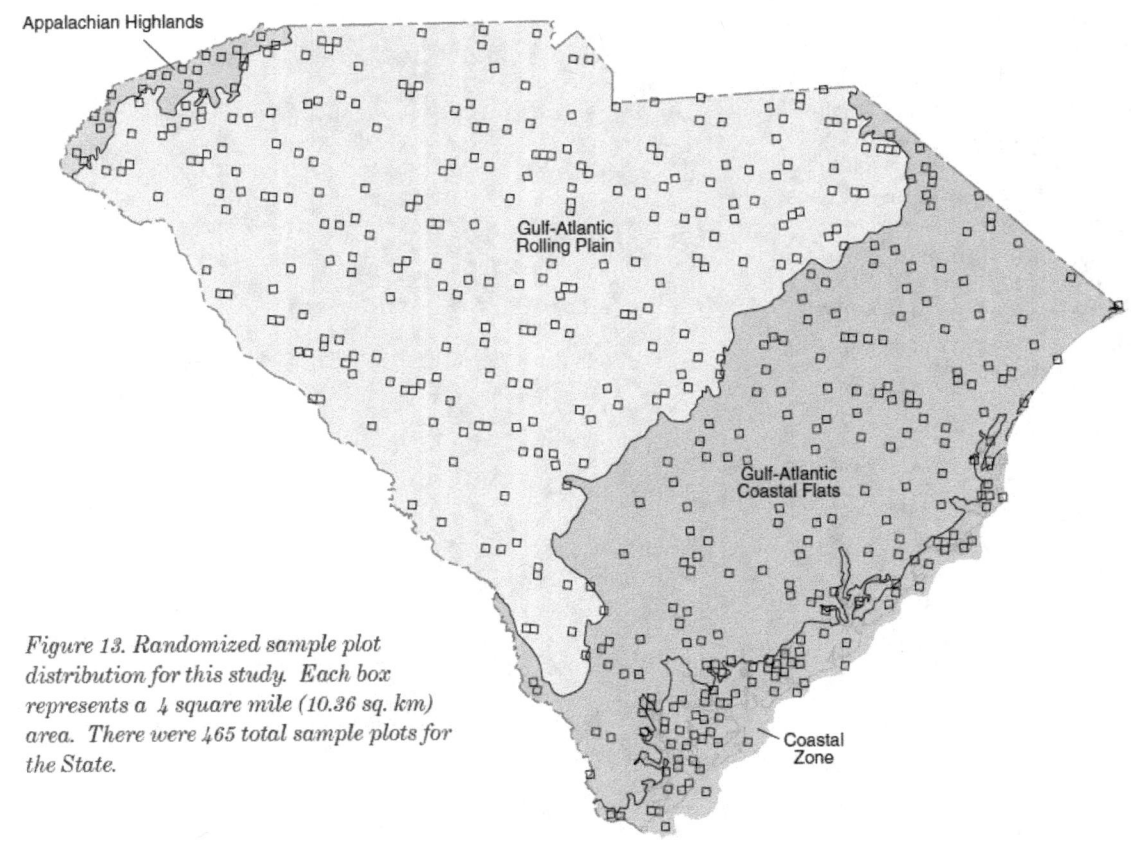

Figure 13. Randomized sample plot distribution for this study. Each box represents a 4 square mile (10.36 sq. km) area. There were 465 total sample plots for the State.

Wetland Types Not Included
In This Study

Because of the limitations of using aerial photography as the primary data source to detect wetlands, certain wet habitats that occur in South Carolina were excluded from this study including:

Small Limesinks or Limestone Sink-holes — These are cavities or depressions that are variable in size and exposure (Nelson 1986). They are associated with partially or completely collapsed limestone rock and can be considered a type of wetland if they hold standing water. Large limesinks or sinkholes would be detected on the aerial photography and included in the study results based on their cover type. However, many lime-sinks are small (less than 1 acre or 0.4 ha), and tree canopies or other vegetation may mask their presence. In these instances, limesinks have been excluded from the report analyses.

Seagrasses or Submerged Aquatic Vegetation — Seagrasses and other submerged plants inhabit the intertidal and subtidal zones of estuaries and near shore coastal waters (Orth *et al.* 1990). The detection of submerged aquatic vegetation is difficult using aerial photography without extensive surface-level observations, tide stage data, water clarity data and low surface waves (Ferguson *et al.* 1993). Because of these requirements, seagrasses were not delineated as part of this study and the data presented in this report are not intended to provide a reliable indicator of the extent of seagrass area in South Carolina's coastal waters.

South Carolina's Wetlands — Common Community Associations

Because the wetland habitat descriptions used in this study are generalized system and class terms from Cowardin *et al.* (1979), further information on the inclusion of some of South Carolina's wetland types is presented in Table 1a–e. This information is organized by physiographic region within the State and is intended to provide a brief physical description or geographic setting, and information on "typical" plant community composition for some of the wetlands encountered in the State. Table 1a–e is not inclusive of all wetland types, communities or plant species that may be found within South Carolina's wetland habitats. Where possible published references documenting similar community descriptions are provided. A complete list of plant species that occur in South Carolina's wetlands is given by Reed (1988).

Ashepoo River wetlands
T. Dahl

Table 1a-e. Wetland habitat descriptions, characteristic plant species and classification designation as found in this study.

Table 1a. Wetland types of South Carolina's Appalachian Highlands (Blue Ridge).

Habitat or Community Type	Description	Characteristic Plant Species	References	Designation for this study
Alder or Rhododendron Thickets	Thick, shady shrub dominated areas on the edges of streams that are occasionally to frequently flooded.	Alder (*Alnus spp.*) Rhododendron (*Rhododendron maximum*) Coastal dog-hobble (*Leucothoe axillaris*) Mountain laurel (*Kalmia latifolia*) Shrubby yellow-root (*Xanthorhiza simplicissima*) Buffalo-nut (*Pyrularia pubera*)	Nelson, 1986	Palustrine Shrub
Coves and Hollows	Wet, mixed mesophytic forest found in valleys or hollows of the Cumberland Plateau and mountainous areas. Only some of these habitats have impaired soil drainage and are considered wetlands.	Yellow-poplar (*Liriodendron tulipifera*) Sweetgum (*Liquidambar styraciflua*) White ash (*Fraxinus americana*) Black cherry (*Prunus serotina*) Black walnut (*Juglans nigra*)	South Carolina Forestry Commission, 1988	Palustrine Forest
Springs and Seeps (Mountain Bog and Fen)	Small, wet areas normally dominated by shrubs or emergents. These small wetlands are usually located in the heads of valleys where the soils are continually saturated.	Common marsh-marigold (*Caltha palustris*) Lamp rush (*Juncus effusus*) Smooth sawgrass (*Cladium mariscoides*) Sedge (*Carex spp.*) Woodland bulrush (*Scirpus expansus*) Sphagnum moss (*Sphagnum spp.*)	Richardson and Gibbons, 1993	Palustrine Emergent
Beaver Ponds	Open water ponds, wet emergent meadows or flooded timber resulting from beaver activity. Although beaver may be found throughout South Carolina, they are most abundant in the Rolling Plain and the Appalachian Highlands regions. Beaver are usually associated with deciduous trees in close proximity to standing or flowing water bodies.	River birch (*Betula nigra*) Red maple (*Acer rubrum*) Yellow poplar (*Liriodendron tulipifera*) Sweetgum (*Liquidambar styraciflua*) Alder (*Alnus spp.*) Swamp cottonwood (*Populus heterophylla*) Willow (*Salix spp.*)	Welsch *et al.*, 1995	Palustrine Forest; Palustrine Shrub; Palustrine Unconsolidated Bottom (ponds)
Freshwater Ponds, Rivers and Lakes	Flowing or standing bodies of freshwater.	Bladderwort (*Utricularia spp.*) Naiad (*Najas guadalupensis*) Pondweed (*Potamogeton spp.*) Water-lily (*Nymphaea odorata*) Yellow pond lily (*Nuphar lutea*) Cattail (*Typha latifolia*) Sedge (*Carex spp.*) Duckweed (*Lemna spp.*)	Aulbach-Smith and de Kozlowski, 1990; Menzel and Cooper, 1992	Palustrine Unconsolidated Bottom (ponds); Lacustrine; Riverine

Table 1b. Wetland types of South Carolina's Gulf-Atlantic Rolling Plain (Piedmont).

Habitat or Community Type	Description	Characteristic Plant Species	References	Designation for this study
Willow Heads and Strands	Woody stands dominated by willow that occur on wet soils adjacent to streams, springs or shallow ponds. These wetlands may also represent the early stages of succession to forest around deep ponds or more permanent water bodies.	Willow (Salix spp.) Alder (Alnus spp.)	Langdon et al., 1981	Palustrine Shrub
Piedmont Seepage Forest	Continually saturated forest on flat areas with closed canopy. Seepage of ground water tends to keep these wetlands saturated year round and distinguishes them from other forested communities.	Red maple (Acer rubrum) Swamp tupelo (Nyssa biflora) Swamp haw (Viburnum cassinoides) Stiff dogwood (Cornus foemina) Poison sumac (Toxicodendron vernix)	Nelson, 1986	Palustrine Forest
Floodplain Forests (red) River Bottoms	Wetlands immediately adjacent to a large drainage system originating in the Piedmont. Sloughs and oxbows extend into low ridges which flood periodically. Soils are characteristically loams or clays.	Water tupelo (Nyssa aquatica) Red maple (Acer rubrum) Black gum (Nyssa sylvatica) Swamp cottonwood (Populus heterophylla) Laurel oak (Quercus laurifolia) Sweetgum (Liquidambar styraciflua) Green ash (Fraxinus pennsylvanica) Water hickory (Carya aquatica) American sycamore (Platanus occidentalis) River birch (Betula nigra) American elm (Ulmus americana) Willow (Salix spp.) Overcup oak (Quercus lyrata)	Barry, 1980; South Carolina Forestry Commission, 1988	Palustrine Forest
Beaver Ponds	See Table 1a.			
Freshwater Ponds, Rivers and Lakes	See Table 1a.			

Table 1c. Wetland types common to both South Carolina's Gulf-Atlantic Rolling Plain (Piedmont) and Coastal Flats.

Habitat Community	Description	Characteristic Plant Species	References	Designation for this study
Bottomland Hardwood (general)	Forested lowland areas that support species that tolerate hydric conditions. Bottomland hardwood wetlands support a predominance of deciduous hardwood tree species, but softwoods may also be represented as well as bald cypress. Bottomlands may exhibit differences in geomorphology, physiography, climate, soils and water characteristics. These differences result in forest associations and types that may be prevalent in one area and not another. Bottomland forested wetlands are characteristically subjected to high water tables, soil saturation, periodic or continuous flooding at various times of the year with water being the dominating environmental factor.	Bald cypress (*Taxodium distichum*) Pond cypress (*Taxodium ascendens*) Water tupelo (*Nyssa aquatica*) Swamp tupelo (*Nyssa biflora*) Water elm (*Planera aquatica*) Swamp privet (*Forestiera acuminata*) Water ash (*Fraxinus caroliniana*) Black willow (*Salix nigra*) Swamp cottonwood (*Populus heterophylla*) Red maple (*Acer rubrum*) Water oak (*Quercus nigra*) Swamp chestnut oak (*Quercus michauxii*) Water hickory (*Carya aquatica*) River birch (*Betula nigra*) Black gum (*Nyssa sylvatica*) Sweet bay (*Magnolia virginiana*) American elm (*Ulmus americana*) Stiff dogwood (*Cornus foemina*) Shagbark hickory (*Carya ovata*) Eastern cottonwood (*Populus deltoides*) Honey-locust (*Gleditsia triacanthos*) Alder (*Alnus serrulata*) Wax myrtle (*Myrica cerifera*) Cabbage palm (*Sabal palmetto*) Sweetgum (*Liquidambar styraciflua*) American sycamore (*Platanus occidentalis*) Possum haw (*Ilex decidua*) Willow oak (*Quercus phellos*) Laurel oak (*Quercus laurifolia*) Southern red oak (*Quercus falcata*) Shumard's oak (*Quercus shumardii*) Loblolly pine (*Pinus taeda*) Common persimmon (*Diospyros virginiana*)	Wharton *et al.*, 1982	Palustrine Forest

Table 1c (continued). Wetland types common to both South Carolina's Gulf-Atlantic Rolling Plain (Piedmont) and Coastal Flats.

Habitat Community	Description	Characteristic Plant Species	References	Designation for this study
Muck Swamps	Deep forested swamps found on predominantly muck soils of silt loam and clay in association with river systems. Many of these swamps have been extensively logged making large tracts rare.	Water tupelo (*Nyssa aquatica*) Bald cypress (*Taxodium distichum*) Black gum (*Nyssa sylvatica*)	Nelson, 1986; South Carolina Forestry Commission, 1988	Palustrine Forest
Peat Swamps	These forested wetlands may be synonymous with pocosins. They support a variety of tree species on peat (organic) soils.	Black gum (*Nyssa sylvatica*) Red maple (*Acer rubrum*) Loblolly pine (*Pinus taeda*) Pond pine (*Pinus serotina*) Atlantic white cedar (*Chamaecyparis thyoides*)	South Carolina Forestry Commission, 1988	Palustrine Forest
Atlantic White Cedar Swamp	Acidic, wet forests dominated by white cedar usually in even-aged stands. Peat tends to accumulate in these nutrient poor wetlands and they support a diverse assemblage of animal species. Within South Carolina Atlantic white cedar stands are reported to occur in Lexington, Kershaw, Chesterfield, Darlington and Marlboro counties.	Atlantic white cedar (*Chamaecyparis thyoides*) Red maple (*Acer rubrum*) Sweet bay (*Magnolia virginiana*) Pond pine (*Pinus serotina*) Red bay (*Persea borbonia*) Bayberry (*Myrica spp.*) Lady's slipper (*Cypripedium acaule*) Cinnamon fern (*Osmunda cinnamomea*) Beak rush (*Rhynchospora spp.*) Golden club (*Orontium aquaticum*) Green arum (*Peltandra virginica*) Sweet pitcherplant (*Sarracenia rubra*) Fetterbush (*Lyonia lucida*) Gallberry (*Ilex spp.*) Blueberry (*Vaccinium spp.*) Swamp titi (*Cyrilla racemiflora*) Laurel-leaf greenbrier (*Smilax laurifolia*) Moss (*Sphagnum spp.*)	Laderman, 1982; 1989; Nelson, 1986	Palustrine Forest

Table 1c (continued). Wetland types common to both South Carolina's Gulf-Atlantic Rolling Plain (Piedmont) and Coastal Flats.

Habitat Community	Description	Characteristic Plant Species	References	Designation for this study
Carolina Bays	Freshwater wetlands within shallow elliptical depressions of unknown origin. Carolina bays are scattered throughout the Coastal Plain and range from less than 50 meters in length to over 8 kilometers. Bays can support wetland plant communities including grasses and sedges (emergent wetlands) to cypress-gum forested swamps. These areas are named for the dominant "bay species" found along drainages of the South Carolina sandhills, slopes and elliptical depressions of the Piedmont and Coastal Plain.	EMERGENT PHASE Maidencane (Panicum hemitomon) Water lily (Nymphaea odorata) Watershield (Brasenia schreberi) Yellow-eyed grass (Xynis spp.) Cinnamon fern (Osmunda cinnamomea) FORESTED PHASE Loblolly bay (Gordonia lasianthus) Pond cypress (Taxodium ascendens) Sweet bay (Magnolia virginiana) Red maple (Acer rubrum) Red bay (Persea borbonia) Pond pine (Pinus serotina) Wax myrtle (Myrica cerifera) Laurel-leaf greenbrier (Smilax laurifolia)	Lide et al., 1995; Richardson and Gibbons, 1993 Sharitz and Gibbons, 1982; Nelson, 1986	Palustrine Emergent Palustrine Shrub
Hillside Bog or Seep	Seasonally or permanently saturated wetlands on slopes of sand hills or other topographic hill-like features of the Piedmont or Coastal Plain. These bogs are dominated by herbaceous species. Insectivorous plants or orchids may be present.	Wiregrass (Aristida spp.) Broom sedge (Andropogon virginicus) Toothache grass (Ctenium aromaticum) Whip nut-rush (Scleria triglomerata) Beak rush (Rhynchospora spp.) Umbrella sedge (Fimbristylis spp.) Yellow pitcherplant (Sarracenia flava) Purple pitcherplant (Sarracenia purpurea) Sweet pitcherplant (Sarracenia rubra) Bladderwort (Utricularia spp.) Sundew (Drosera spp.) Rose pogonia (Pogonia ophioglossoides) Ladies' tresses (Spiranthes spp.) Moss (Sphagnum spp.)	Nelson, 1986	Palustrine Emergent
Freshwater Emergent Marshes (deep and shallow)	These are the most common type of wetland dominated by grasses and sedges. These areas usually occupy topographic depressions, swales or the margins of ponds, lakes or rivers. These wetlands are species rich and include grasses, sedges, annual weeds and shrubs. Water levels vary from permanent standing water to wet meadow (saturated) conditions. Some freshwater marshes near the outer Coastal Plain may be tidally flooded.	Cattail (Typha spp.) Maidencane (Panicum hemitomon) Wild rice (Zizania aquatica) Common reed (Phragmites australis) Sedge (Carex spp.) Bulrush (Scirpus spp.) Rush (Juncus spp.)	Aulbach-Smith and de Kozlowski, 1990	Palustrine Emergent

Table 1d. Wetland types of South Carolina's Coastal Flats.

Habitat Community	Description	Characteristic Plant Species	References	Designation for this study
Blackwater or Brownwater River Bottoms (includes swamp cane islands)	Wetlands occurring in the floodplain of a major drainage or river system originating in the Coastal Plain.	Sweetgum (*Liquidambar styraciflua*) Loblolly pine (*Pinus taeda*) Sugarberry (*Celtis laevigata*) Overcup oak (*Quercus lyrata*) Water oak (*Quercus nigra*) Willow oak (*Quercus phellos*) Laurel oak (*Quercus laurifolia*) White ash (*Fraxinus americana*) American sycamore (*Platanus occidentalis*) American holly (*Ilex opaca*) American elm (*Ulmus americana*)	Nelson, 1986	Palustrine Forest
Beech-Magnolia Hammock	These forests usually have calcareous soils and are dominated by a number of hardwood species. Flooding is not as evident as in the river bottoms but represents a wet variation of the mixed hardwood forest type.	Beech (*Fagus grandifolia*) Southern magnolia (*Magnolia grandiflora*) Sweetgum (*Liquidambar styraciflua*) Spruce pine (*Pinus glabra*) Laurel oak (*Quercus laurifolia*) American holly (*Ilex opaca*) Pignut hickory (*Carya glabra*) Red hickory (*Carya ovatis*)	Nelson, 1986	Palustrine Forest
Non-Riverine Swamp Forest / Cypress or Gum Ponds	Depressional forested wetlands on poorly drained lowlands that are not associated with riverine systems. These wetlands usually maintain some surface water and provide important wildlife habitat.	Pond cypress (*Taxodium ascendens*) Bald cypress (*Taxodium distichum*) Black gum (*Nyssa sylvatica*) Red maple (*Acer rubrum*) Dahoon (*Ilex cassine*) Sweetgum (*Liquidambar styraciflua*) Swamp chestnut oak (*Quercus michauxii*) Pond pine (*Pinus serotina*)	Nelson, 1986	Palustrine Forest
Pine Flatwoods	Forested wetland on flat or slightly undulating terrain dominated by moisture tolerant pine trees. Soils in these areas are usually sandy with a characteristically high water table. Not all pine flatwood communities may be wetland.	Longleaf pine (*Pinus palustris*) Loblolly pine (*Pinus taeda*) Slash pine (*Pinus elliottii*) Blackjack oak (*Quercus marilandica*) Bitter gallberry (*Ilex glabra*) Arrow-wood (*Viburnum spp.*) Bluestem (*Andropogon spp.*) Wiregrass (*Aristida spp.*)	Nelson, 1986	Palustrine Forest

Table 1d (continued). Wetland types of South Carolina's Coastal Flats.

Habitat Community	Description	Characteristic Plant Species	References	Designation for this study
Pine Savannah	Forested phase of the pitcher plant bog. This type of wetland community occurs in flat areas of the Coastal Plain and usually supports many herbaceous species in the understory.	Longleaf pine (*Pinus palustris*) Pond pine (*Pinus serotina*) Wiregrass (*Aristida spp.*) Toothache grass (*Ctenium aromaticum*) Purple silkyscale (*Anthaenantia rufa*) Nut-rush (*Scleria spp.*) Yellow pitcherplant (*Sarracenia flava*) Sundew (*Drosera spp.*)	Nelson, 1986	Palustrine Forest or Palustrine Shrub
Pocosin	Low, wet forest or shrub dominated community that develops on saturated, nutrient poor, organic soils (peat) of the Coastal Plain.	Pond pine (*Pinus serotina*) Loblolly bay (*Gordonia lasianthus*) Pond cypress (*Taxodium ascendens*) Swamp tupelo (*Nyssa biflora*) Red bay (*Persea borbonia*) Sweet bay (*Magnolia virginiana*) Wax myrtle (*Myrica cerifera*) Red maple (*Acer rubrum*) Dahoon (*Ilex cassine*) Fetterbush (*Lyonia lucida*) Greenbrier (*Smilax spp.*) Bitter gallberry (*Ilex glabra*) Blueberry (*Vaccinium spp.*) Huckleberry (*Gaylussacia spp.*) Large gallberry (*Ilex coriacea*) Choke cherry (*Aronia arbutifolia*) Poison ivy (*Toxicodendron radicans*)	Jones, 1981; Langdon et al., 1981	Palustrine Shrub
Wet Flats (low)	Characterized by non-alluvial soils with higher fertility, these wetlands can be found on abandoned rice fields within South Carolina's Coastal Plain.	Sweetgum (*Liquidambar styraciflua*) Red maple (*Acer rubrum*) Water oak (*Quercus nigra*) Laurel oak (*Quercus laurifolia*) Willow oak (*Quercus phellos*) Ash (*Fraxinus spp.*) Loblolly pine (*Pinus taeda*) Elm (*Ulmus spp.*)	South Carolina Forestry Commission, 1988	Palustrine Forest
Wet Flats (high)	Non-alluvial soils with better drainage.	Cherry-bark oak (*Quercus pagoda*) Shumard's oak (*Quercus shumardii*) Swamp chestnut oak ((*Quercus michauxii*) Yellow poplar (*Liriodendron tulipifera*) Hickory (*Carya spp.*) Beech (*Fagus spp.*)	South Carolina Forestry Commission, 1988	Palustrine Forest

Table 1e. Wetland types of South Carolina's Coastal Zone.

Habitat Community	Description	Characteristic Plant Species	References	Designation for this study
Salt Flat or Beach	Coastal flats or beaches are composed of mud or sand found in hyper-saline conditions along the coast or on the landward side of barrier islands.	Coastal saltgrass (*Distichlis spicata*) Annual seepweed (*Suaeda linearis*) Virginia glasswort (*Salicornia virginica*) Carolina sea-lavender (*Limonium carolinianum*) Pit-seed goosefoot (*Chenopodium berlandieri*) Halberd-leaf saltbush (*Atriplex patula*) Perennial saltmarsh aster (*Aster tenuifolius*) Seashore dropseed (*Sporobolus virginicus*)	Nelson, 1986	Estuarine Shore
Interdunal Pond	These are freshwater ponds or swales formed between beach ridges or dunes of the outer Coastal Zone or on barrier islands. Although these areas are freshwater communities, the salinity of these wetlands can vary with tidal connection and periodicity of flooding.	Carolina mosquito fern (*Azolla caroliniana*) Duckweed (*Lemna spp.*) Bogmat (*Wolffiella floridana*) Coastal marsh-pennywort (*Hydrocotyle bonariensis*) Cattail (*Typha spp.*) Sawgrass (*Cladium jamaicense*) Pondweed (*Potamogeton spp.*) Climbing hempvine (*Mikania scandens*)	Nelson, 1986	Palustrine Unconsolidated Bottom (ponds)
Salt Marsh	These are estuarine emergent wetlands that occur along flat, tidally influenced areas of the coastline or barrier islands. Salt marshes are regularly flooded by the tides and are dominated by relatively few salt tolerant grasses. Salt marshes are some of the most commonly recognized wetlands and support a variety of wildlife, fish and shellfish.	Saltmarsh cordgrass (*Spartina alterniflora*) Saltmeadow cordgrass (*Spartina patens*) Coastal saltgrass (*Distichlis spicata*) Black needlerush (*Juncus roemerianus*)	Barry, 1980; South Carolina Coastal Council, 1982	Estuarine Emergent
Brackish Marsh	Brackish marshes are found on the upland side or edges of estuaries, tidal creeks or salt marshes. Salinity is lower than in salt marshes as a result of salt and fresh water mixing at the interface of the estuarine and freshwater systems. These wetlands are often dominated by a few plant species, most notably Black needlerush (*Juncus roemerianus*).	Black needlerush (*Juncus roemerianus*) Big cordgrass (*Spartina cynosuroides*) Saltmeadow cordgrass (*Spartina patens*) Seaside bulrush (*Scirpus robustus*) Swordgrass (*Scirpus americanus*) Little-head spike-rush (*Eleocharis parvula*) Coastal saltgrass (*Distichlis spicata*) Cattail (*Typha spp.*) Arrowhead (*Sagittaria spp.*)	Barry, 1980; Nelson, 1986	Estuarine Emergent or Palustrine Emergent

Results: Status, Distribution and Ownership of Wetlands

South Carolina had an estimated 4,104,850 acres (1,661,880 ha) of wetlands in 1989. Of this area, 89 percent were freshwater, and 11 percent were estuarine (saltwater) wetlands. The temporal and spatial changes of wetland area are presented in Appendix B. Wetland area in relation to the total land area of South Carolina and wetland area by system type is presented in Figure 14 a–d.

Estuarine emergent wetlands are dominated by salt-tolerant plants (Cowardin *et al.* 1979). In 1989, an estimated 93 percent of South Carolina's estuarine wetlands by area were emergent (Figure 15). An additional six percent of the area of all estuarine wetlands were tidal flats, beaches or shorelines and one percent was dominated by estuarine shrubs. The distribution of estuarine emergent wetlands along South Carolina's coast is shown in Figure 16. The mean size of the estuarine emergent marshes sampled was 71 acres (28.7 ha). The mean size of estuarine shrub wetlands was much smaller, 3

acres (1.2 ha). Estuarine beaches, exposed flats or shorelines averaged 11 acres (4.5 ha) based on those areas sampled as part of this study.

Almost all estuarine wetlands were found in the Coastal Zone (97 percent). However, a small portion of estuarine wetlands (3 percent) were found to extend into the Coastal Flats physiographic region along the reaches of tidal inlets and rivers.

Within the Coastal Zone the mean size of the estuarine wetlands sampled was 68 acres (27.5 ha). Fifteen percent of all vegetated estuarine wetlands were adjacent to urban landscapes. This percentage was composed primarily of the salt marshes near Myrtle Beach, Charleston, Seabrook Island, Hilton Head and Savannah. An additional 21 percent of South Carolina's estuarine wetlands were adjacent to agricultural lands, while 57 percent were adjacent to undeveloped lands.

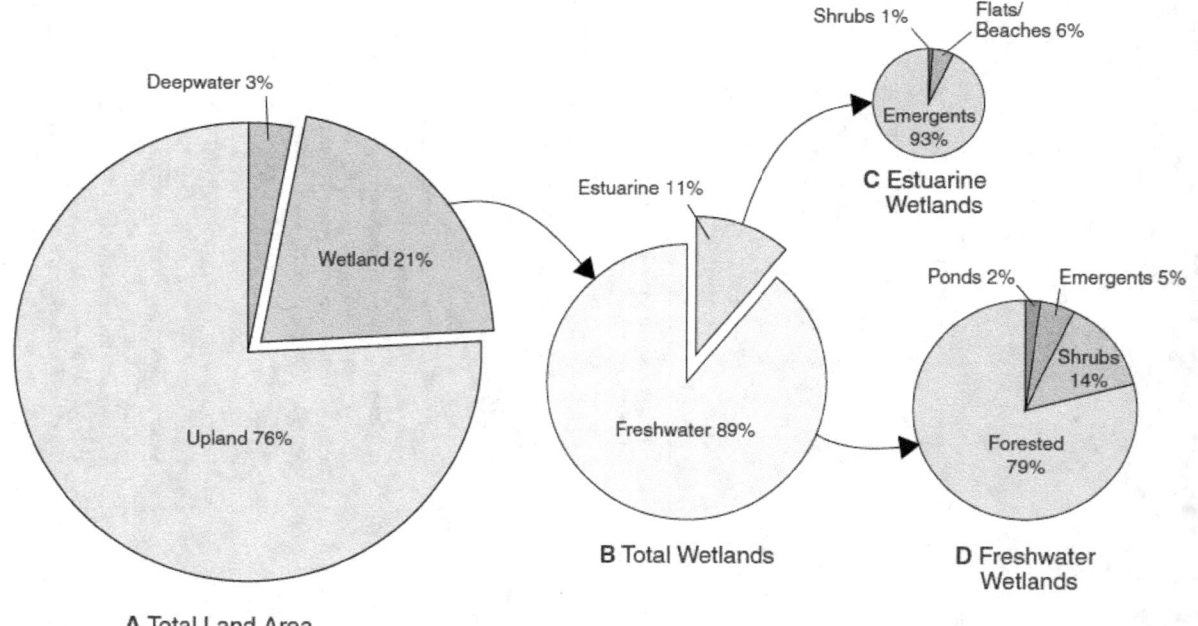

Figure 14 A–D. Wetland area (A) as compared to total area of the State; (B) percent by estuarine and freshwater types; (C) estuarine covertypes; (D) freshwater covertypes.

Figure 15. Estuarine emergent wetlands along South Carolina's coast.

There were slightly more than 3.6 million acres (1,457,490 ha) of freshwater wetlands in the State in 1989. Forested wetlands were most prevalent, making up 79 percent of all freshwater wetlands, or almost 2.9 million acres (1,174,089 ha). Forested wetlands averaged 25 acres in size (10.1 ha), the largest mean size in area of all freshwater wetland types.

The distribution of palustrine wetlands by physiographic region is shown in

Table 2. The majority of freshwater wetland area was found in the Coastal Flats (61 percent). The Rolling Plain contained 36 percent of all freshwater wetlands by area. The Coastal Zone and Appalachian Highlands had 2 and 1 percent, respectively (Figure 17). More detailed information about the distribution of wetlands by covertype within physiographic regions of the State is shown in Table 3.

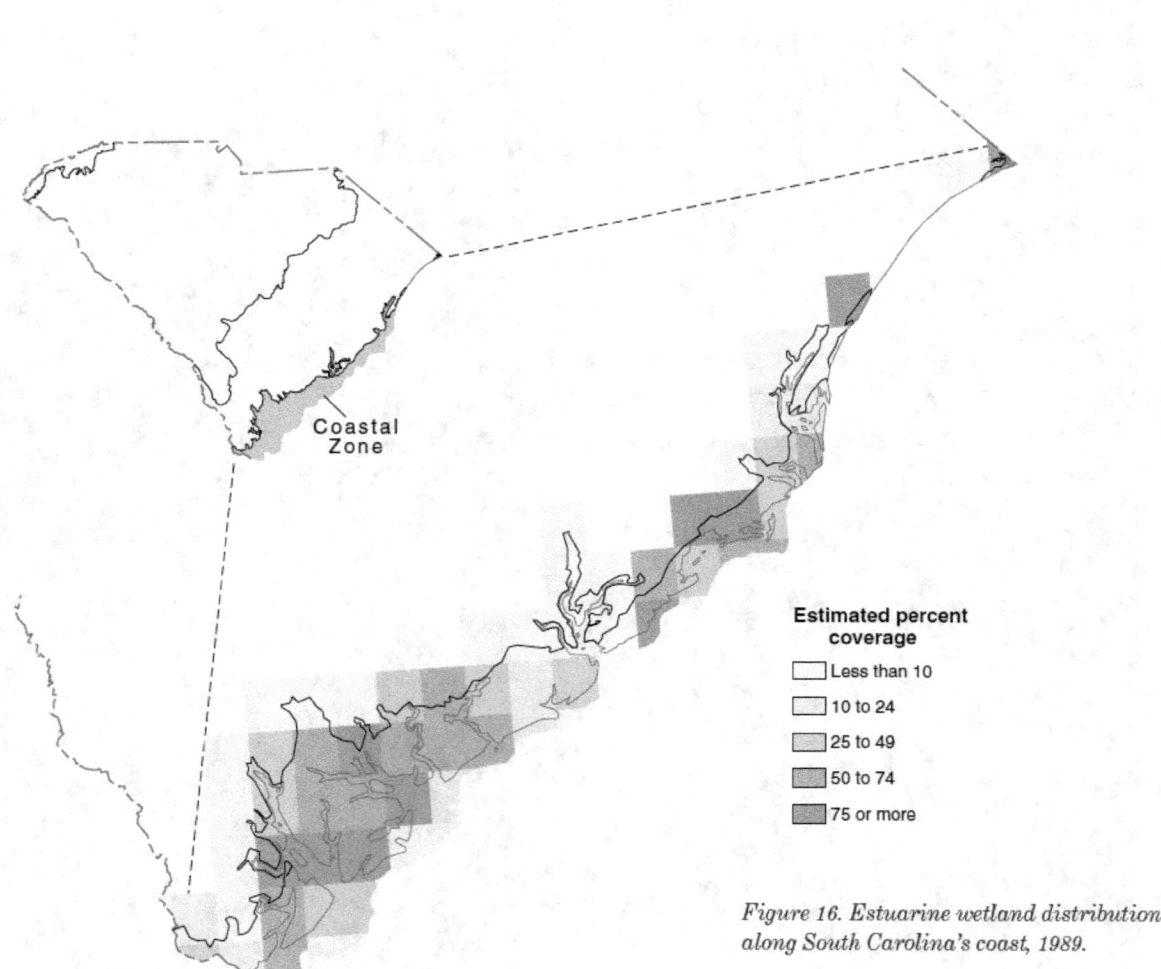

Estimated percent coverage

☐ Less than 10
☐ 10 to 24
☐ 25 to 49
☐ 50 to 74
☐ 75 or more

Figure 16. Estuarine wetland distribution along South Carolina's coast, 1989.

Table 2. Distribution of all palustrine wetland types by physiographic region in South Carolina as found in this study, 1989.

Physiographic Region	Estimated Area in Acres		Percent CV[1]	Percent of Total Palustrine
Appalachian Highlands	2,351	(951.8 ha)	19	<1
Gulf Atlantic Rolling Plain	1,343,250	(543,826 ha)	9	36
Gulf Atlantic Coastal Flats	2,251,375	(911,488 ha)	5	61
Coastal Zone	64,430	(26,085 ha)	19	2
Total Palustrine	**3,661,406**	**(1,482,351 ha)**	**5**	**100**

[1]*Percent coefficient of variation is expressed as (standard deviation/mean) ∗ (100).*

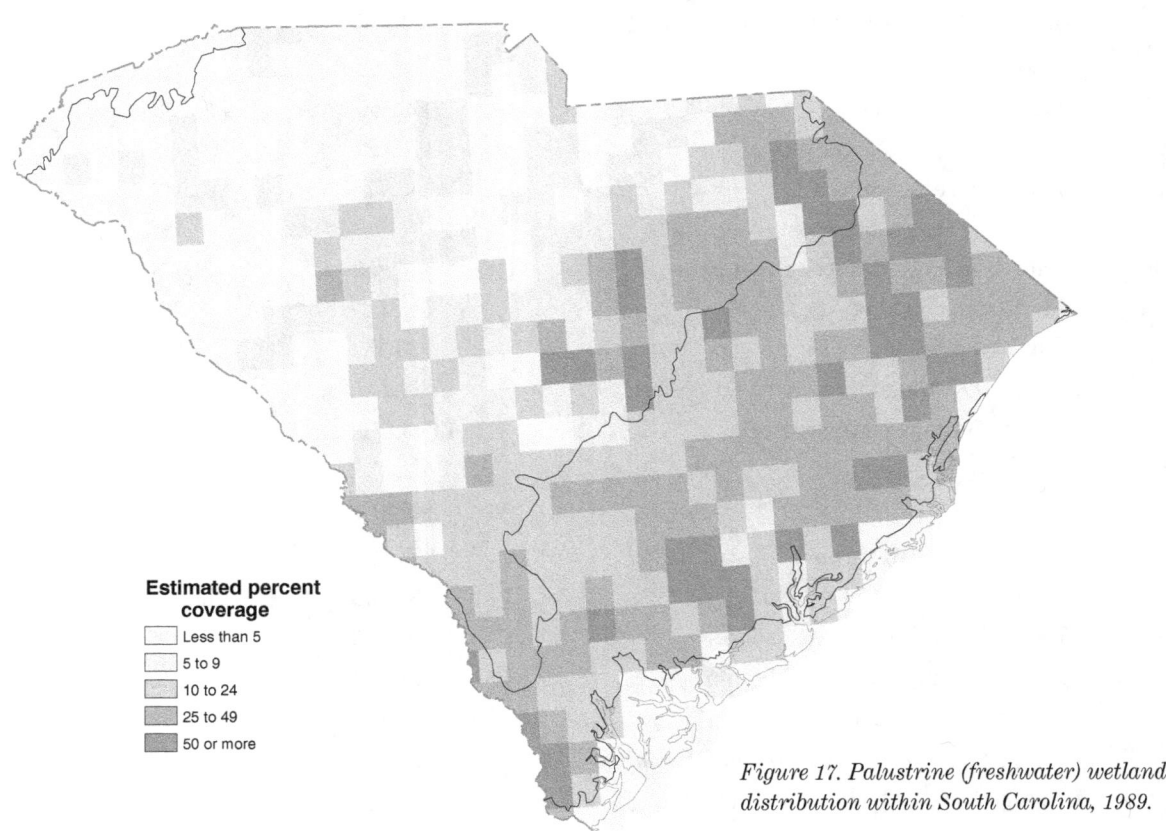

Estimated percent coverage

- Less than 5
- 5 to 9
- 10 to 24
- 25 to 49
- 50 or more

Figure 17. Palustrine (freshwater) wetland distribution within South Carolina, 1989.

Table 3. Estimated acreage of wetlands by covertype classes within the physiographic regions of South Carolina, 1989.

| Wetland Type | 1989 Area | | Percent CV[1] |
	Acres	Hectares	
Appalachian Highlands			
Palustrine forested	1,162	471	34
Palustrine scrub/shrub	329	133	34
Palustrine emergent	313	127	50
Palustrine unconsolidated shore			
Palustrine unconsolidated bottom	547	222	28
Palustrine aquatic bed			
Total Palustrine wetland area for region	*2,351*	*952*	*19*
Total wetland area for region	**2,351**	**952**	**19**
Atlantic Rolling Plain			
Palustrine forested	1,056,350	427,822	10
Palustrine scrub/shrub	170,422	69,021	16
Palustrine emergent	45,778	18,540	13
Palustrine unconsolidated shore	484	196	34
Palustrine unconsolidated bottom	55,859	22,623	7
Palustrine aquatic bed	927	375	42
Palustrine farmed	13,430	5,437	22
Total Palustrine wetland area for region	*1,343,250*	*543,826*	*9*
Total wetland area for region	**1,343,250**	**543,826**	**9**
Atlantic Coastal Flats			
Palustrine forested	1,793,315	726,292	6
Palustrine scrub/shrub	337,883	136,843	14
Palustrine emergent	97,405	39,449	19
Palustrine unconsolidated shore	237	96	55
Palustrine unconsolidated bottom	21,362	8,652	14
Palustrine aquatic bed	1,173	475	31
Total Palustrine wetland area for region	*2,251,375*	*911,807*	*5*
Estuarine intertidal scrub/shrub	859	348	61
Estuarine intertidal emergent	42,318	17,139	57
Estuarine intertidal unconsolidated shore			
Total Estuarine wetland area for region	*43,177*	*17,487*	*56*
Total wetland area for region	**2,294,552**	**929,294**	**5**

Table 3 (continued). Estimated acreage of wetlands by covertype classes within the physiographic regions of South Carolina, 1989.

Wetland Type	1989 Area		Percent CV
	Acres	Hectares	
Coastal Zone			
Palustrine forested	32,238	13,056	22
Palustrine scrub/shrub	4,649	1,883	24
Palustrine emergent	23,899	9,679	41
Palustrine unconsolidated shore	505	205	55
Palustrine unconsolidated bottom	3,057	1,238	20
Palustrine aquatic bed	82	33	44
Total Palustrine wetland area for region	*64,430*	*26,094*	*19*
Estuarine intertidal scrub/shrub	2,912	1,179	23
Estuarine intertidal emergent	368,928	149,416	10
Estuarine intertidal unconsolidated shore	26,324	10,661	21
Total Estuarine wetland area for region	*398,164*	*161,256*	*8*
Marine intertidal unconsolidated shore	2,103	852	35
Total Marine wetland area for region	*2,103*	*852*	*35*
Total wetland area for region	**464,697**	**188,202**	**6**
South Carolina			
Palustrine forested	2,883,065	1,167,641	5
Palustrine scrub/shrub	513,283	207,880	10
Palustrine emergent	167,395	67,795	13
Palustrine unconsolidated shore	1,226	497	29
Palustrine unconsolidated bottom	80,825	32,735	6
Palustrine aquatic bed	2,182	883	24
Palustrine farmed	13,430	5,439	22
Total Palustrine wetland area for state	*3,661,406*	*1,482,870*	*5*
Estuarine intertidal scrub/shrub	3,771	1,527	22
Estuarine intertidal emergent	411,246	166,555	9
Estuarine intertidal unconsolidated shore	26,324	10,661	21
Total Estuarine wetland area for state	*441,341*	*178,743*	*9*
Marine intertidal unconsolidated shore	2,103	852	35
Total Marine wetland area for state	*2,103*	*852*	*35*
Total wetland area for state	**4,104,850**	**1,662,465**	**4**

[1]*Percent coefficient of variation is expressed as (standard deviation/mean) * (100).*

Wetlands dominated by shrubs (including tree species under 6 m in height) made up an estimated 14 percent of the freshwater wetlands. Freshwater emergent marshes and ponds composed five and two percent of the area respectively. Shrub wetlands averaged 9 acres (3.6 ha) in size, freshwater emergent marshes averaged 5 acres (2.0 ha) and ponds 2 acres (0.8 ha). The average size and range by freshwater wetland types are presented in Table 4.

The concentration of forested wetlands in the coastal region and the relationship between the major river systems in the formation and maintenance of South Carolina's forested wetlands is illustrated in Figure 18. Bottomland hardwood communities located along the major river flood plains make up a substantial portion of South Carolina's wetland area. Figure 19 illustrates South Carolina's wetlands in relation to the State's physiographic regions and major river systems. By comparison, relatively few freshwater wetlands are located in or adjacent to larger lakes. About 4.6 percent of all palustrine wetlands are directly adjacent to lacustrine systems.

Freshwater wetlands are also less common in urban landscapes. Approximately 8.4 percent of South Carolina's palustrine wetlands are in or adjacent to urban areas as identified by this study. The majority of palustrine wetlands (55 percent) are found in or adjacent to agricultural lands.

The 4,104,850 acres (1,661,880 ha) of wetlands in South Carolina make up approximately 21 percent of the land surface area of the State. An additional 3 percent of the surface area or 655,700 acres (265,466 ha), are deepwater habitats. About 10 percent of the total land area in South Carolina is in public (State or Federal) ownership. Federal land holdings include 1,198,600 acres (485,263 ha) and the State owns another 825,700 acres (334,290 ha).

About 17.1 percent of the Federal land holdings are wetlands. This is approximately 5.0 percent of South Carolina's total wetland acreage. Another 14.7 percent of the State-owned lands are wetland, or about 2.9 percent of the State's total wetland area. Over 91.0 percent of South Carolina's wetland acreage is in private ownership. Table 5 details the wetland area by respective reserves and publicly-owned units within the State.

Table 4. Average area and size range of palustrine wetlands as they appeared within the sample units for South Carolina in 1989.

Wetland Type	Mean (acres)	Range (acres)
Palustrine forest	25 (10.0 ha)	<1 to >2200 (0.4 – 891 ha)
Palustrine shrub	9 (3.6 ha)	<1 to >1600 (0.4 – 648 ha)
Palustrine emergent	5 (2.0 ha)	<1 to >1300 (0.4 – 526 ha)
Freshwater ponds	2 (0.8 ha)	<1 to >20 (0.4 – 8.1 ha)
Other misc. types	2 – 3 (0.8 – 1.2 ha)	<1 to >17 (0.4 – 6.9 ha)

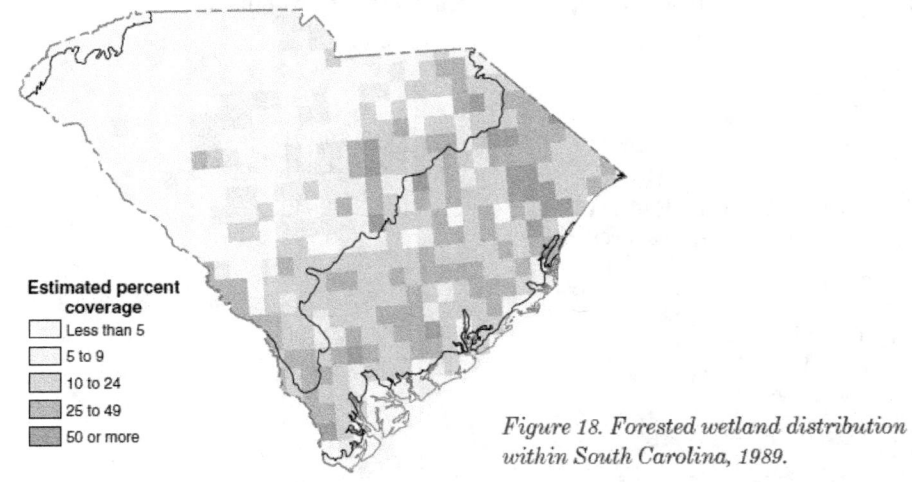

Estimated percent coverage

Less than 5
5 to 9
10 to 24
25 to 49
50 or more

Figure 18. Forested wetland distribution within South Carolina, 1989.

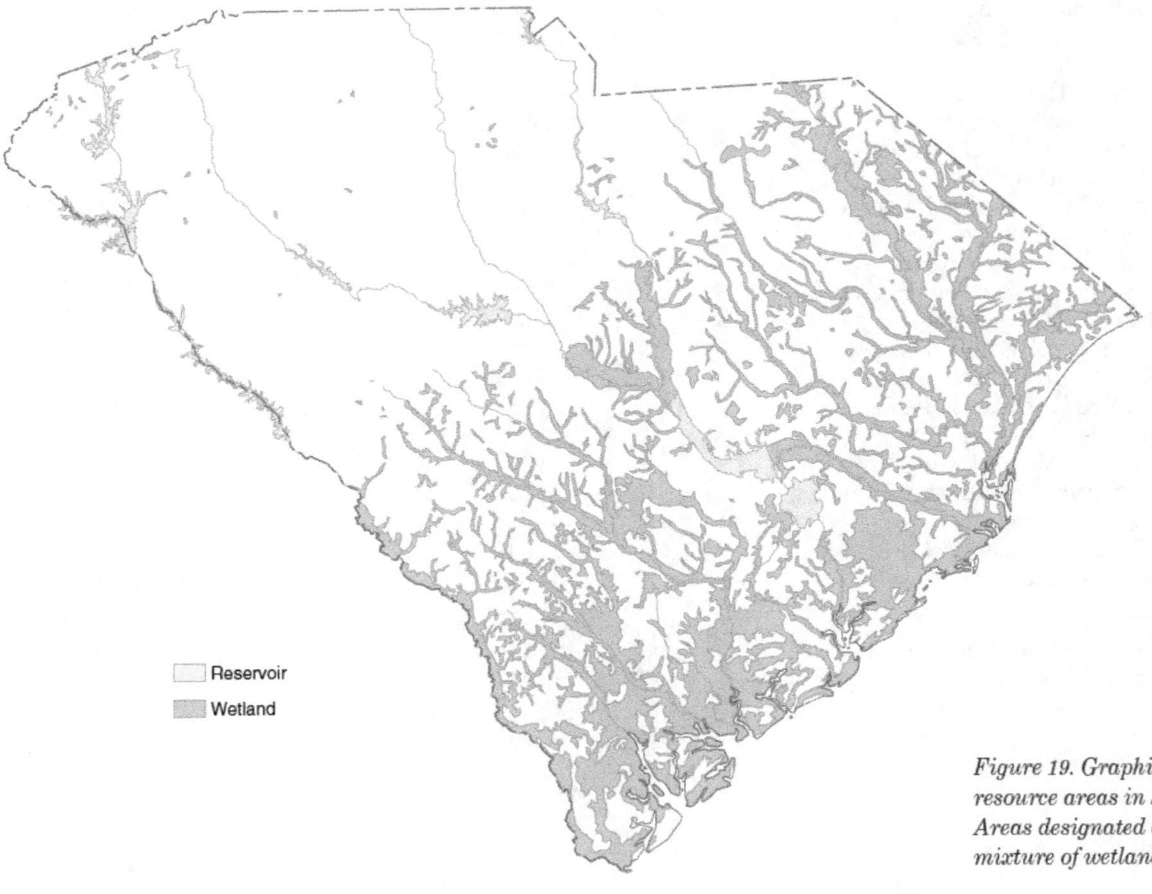

Reservoir
Wetland

Figure 19. Graphic representation of wetland resource areas in South Carolina, 1989. Areas designated as wetland may represent a mixture of wetland and uplands.

Table 5. Area of reserves and publicly-owned lands that may contain wetlands in South Carolina.

Land Ownership   *Wetland Acres*

SOUTH CAROLINA - STATE LANDS

South Carolina Park System	15,151
	1,481 (lakes)
ACE Basin National Estuarine Research Reserve	11,942
North Inlet/Winyah National Estuarine Research Reserve	9,000

Heritage Trust Preserves - SC

Capers Island	2,100
Tom Yawkey Complex	17,700
Stevens Creek Natural Area	------
Eastatoe Creek Gorge	373
Bird Key-Stono	20
Victoria Bluff	1,111
Crosby Oxypolis Heritage Preserve	32
Colleton County Cowbane Preserve	32
Nipper Creek	68
Watson Tract	1,660
Bunched Arrowhead	178
Ashmore Tract	529
Cathedral Bay	58
Flat Creek/40 Acre Rock	1,436
Cartwheel Bay	568
Savannah River Bluffs	------
Tillman Sand Ridge	------
Savage Bay	77
Bennett's Bay	679
Tilghman Heritage Preserve	456
Chandler Heritage Preserve	251
Snee Farm Heritage Preserve	------
Buzzard Roost Heritage Preserve	------
Dargan Heritage Preserve	2,387
Shealy's Pond Heritage Preserve	62
Woods Bay Heritage Preserve	368
Lewis Ocean Bay Heritage Preserve	9,343
Glassy Mountain Heritage Preserve	------
Deveaux Bank Heritage Preserve	15
Waccamaw Bridges Heritage Preserve	453
Janet Harrison Highpond Heritage Preserve	30
St. Helena Sound Heritage Preserve	7,536
Little Pee Dee River Heritage Preserve	3,771
Great Pee Dee River Heritage Preserve	2,725
Little Pee Dee State Park Bay	301
Little Pee Dee (Ward) Heritage Preserve	269
Lynchburg Savannah Heritage Preserve	275
Pacolet River Heritage	-------
Segars Heritage Preserve	400
Henderson Heritage Preserve	-------

Wildlife Management Areas

Bear Island Wildlife Management Area	12,055
Donnelley Wildlife Management Area	8,048
State University System	8,100
State Owned Subtotal	121,040

Table 5 (continued). Area of reserves and publicly-owned lands that may contain wetlands in South Carolina.

Land Ownership	Wetland Acres
SOUTH CAROLINA -FEDERAL LANDS	
Department of Agriculture	
Forest Service	
Francis Marion NF	
Hell Hole Bay	2,125
Wambaw Creek	912
Wambaw Swamp	4,815
Little Wambaw Swamp	5,047
Remaining Forest Areas	27,101
Sumter NF	1,500
Department of Energy	
Savannah River Facility	39,500
Department Interior	
Park Service	
Congaree Swamp Natl. Monument	15,138
Fish and Wildlife Service	
Cape Romain NWR	60,745
Carolina Sandhills NWR	2,736
Santee NWR	10,425
Pinckney Island	2,795
Savannah NWR (SC portion)	9,323
	4,900 (lakes)
ACE Basin NWR	11,942
Department of Defense	
Charleston Naval Weapons Station	2,795
Shaw Air Force Base	3,074
Other Defense Installations	------
Federally Owned Subtotal	204,873
AUDUBON SANCTUARIES	
Francis Beidler Forest	5,819
Silver Bluff Plantation	3,100
Medway Plantation	821
Alexander Sprunt, Jr.	640
McAlhany Sanctuary	370
Heritage Trust Bunched Arrowhead Preserve	140
Audubon-Newhall Nature Preserve	------
Parson's Mountain Recreation Area	------
THE NATURE CONSERVANCY	
Great Swamp and Ivanhoe Tract	473
Other holdings	7,974
Conservation Organization Subtotal	19,337
Estimated total acreage	345,250

Sources: Bebber 1988; Brunswig and Lake1991; Kane and Keeton1993; U.S. Fish and Wildlife Service1994 (b) and (c).

Wetlands Trends, 1982–1989

The average annual net loss of wetlands observed was 2,920 acres (1,182 ha). Total wetland area in South Carolina declined by 0.5 percent from 1982 and 1989. Palustrine forested wetlands suffered the biggest losses, declining 5.1 percent over the study period. Palustrine shrub wetlands realized the largest gains, increasing by 33.4 percent (Table 6).

Loss of estuarine wetlands was minimal. Estuarine wetlands declined 109 acres (44 ha) during the seven year time frame between 1982 and 1989. The average annual loss of estuarine wetlands was 17 acres (6.9 ha). It is believed that these minor losses were the result of coastal erosion processes as estuarine wetlands were converted to deep water.

Almost all of South Carolina's wetland losses were to freshwater classes. Freshwater (palustrine) forested wetlands declined by an estimated 155,500 acres (62,956 ha). Of this total change, 13,200 forested wetland acres (5,344 ha) were lost to upland land uses. Another 2,650 acres (1073 ha) were converted to lacustrine deepwater through the creation of impoundments or flooding, while 136,500 acres (55,263 ha) were converted to other vegetated types that remained as wetland.

Palustrine wetlands declined by 18,800 acres (7,611 ha) from 1982–1989. An estimated 16,900 acres (6,840 ha) were lost to upland land uses. Overall this represents an annual loss of 2,920 acres (1,182 ha) of vegetated freshwater wetlands. Loss of vegetated wetlands was partially offset by the addition of open water ponds. Pond area increased by 10.5 percent (8,450 acres or 3,421 ha). Almost half (45 percent) of this area came at the expense of other wetland types.

Three major activities contributed to the loss of freshwater wetlands to uplands: Agriculture converted an estimated 5,210 acres (2,109 ha) to upland, and an additional 1,100 acres (445 ha) to farmed wetlands. Forestry converted 5,890 acres (2,385 ha) of wetlands to uplands, and urbanization was responsible for 4,113 acres (1,665 ha) of wetland loss.

Collectively, agriculture, forestry and urbanization were responsible for 81 percent of all the freshwater wetland losses between 1982 and 1989. Agricultural conversions (exclusive of farmed wetlands) accounted for 28 percent, forestry 31 percent and urban expansion 22 percent respectively. The remaining losses of freshwater wetlands to uplands were caused by rural development, (9 percent or 1700 acres [688 ha]), (Figure 20).

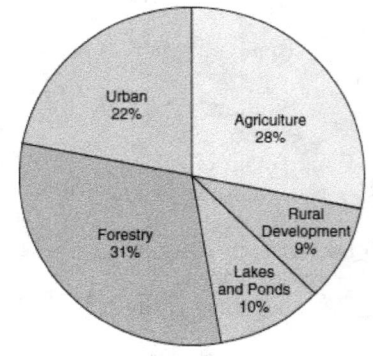

Figure 20. Change in wetlands (as a percentage) converted to various land uses in South Carolina between 1982 and 1989.

Although losses of wetlands to agriculture were observed in each physiographic region of the state the majority of agricultural conversions of wetlands occurred in the Coastal Flats and the Rolling Plain (Piedmont). Conversion of wetlands to silvicultural land use was primarily restricted to the Coastal Flats. The conversion of forested wetlands to other wetland types (shrubs or emergents), occurred uniformly across the state with the exception of the Appalachian Highlands. These activities had a major impact on forested wetland resources (Figure 21).

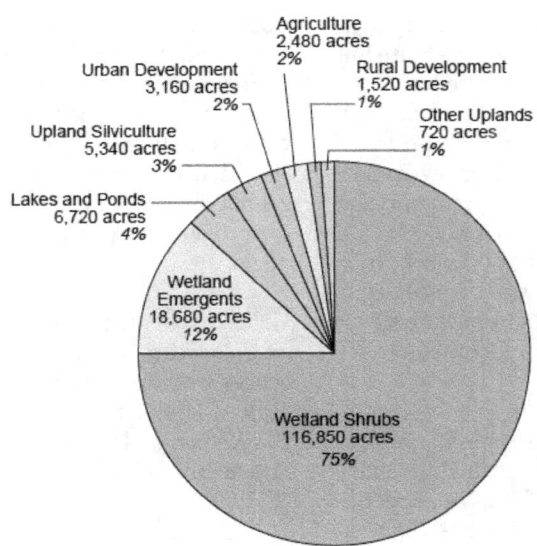

Figure 21. Conversion and loss of forested wetland in South Carolina, 1982-1989. This graphic portrays both losses to upland land uses as well as conversion of forested wetlands to other wetland types.

Table 6. Estimated wetland area in South Carolina in 1982 and 1989 and the change(s) as reported for various categories in this study.

Wetland Type	1982 Area in Acres	1989 Area in Acres	Change in Acres	Percent Change
Estuarine Non-Vegetated	28,262 (19)	28,426 (19)	+165 (363)	0.6
Estuarine Vegetated	415,291 (9)	415,017 (9)	-274 (137)	-0.1
All Estuarine Wetlands	443,553 (9)	443,444 (9)	-109 (729)	0.0
Palustrine Non Vegetated	73,490 (6)	82,050 (6)	+8,560 (15)	11.6
Palustrine Emergent	169,610 (13)	167,395 (13)	-2,214 (519)	-1.3
Palustrine Scrub/Shrub	384,864 (14)	513,283 (10)	+128,419 (22)	33.4
Palustrine Forested	3,038,551 (5)	2,883,066 (5)	-155,485 (16)	-5.1
Palustrine Vegetated	3,606,706 (5)	3,579,356 (5)	-27,350 (17)	-0.8
All Palustrine Wetlands	3,680,196 (4)	3,661,406 (5)	-18,790 (24)	-0.5
All Wetlands	4,123,749 (4)	4,104,850 (4)	-18,899 (25)	-0.5

*( ) Percent coefficient of variation. Percent coefficient of variation is expressed as (standard deviation/mean) * (100).*

Rural development was concentrated in the Rolling Plain portion of the state but this change in land use resulted in comparatively small losses of palustrine wetland area. The possible exception is Horry County where rapid growth and development appeared to be expanding the incorporated regions as well as affecting the rural areas of the county. Here, the loss of freshwater wetlands to unidentified or miscellaneous "other" upland land uses was predominant (Figure 22).

Agricultural losses were the only effects observed in the Appalachian Highlands. Clearly the majority of land use actions affecting wetland area changes occurred in the Gulf-Atlantic Rolling Plain and the Coastal Flats. Agriculture and some rural development activities affected the Rolling Plain while agriculture, forestry, urbanization and miscellaneous other upland land uses affected the Coastal Flats.

Losses of wetlands between 1982 and 1989 in South Carolina occurred outside of Federal lands (Figure 23) and on the outskirts of metropolitan areas. There were no confirmed losses of wetland recorded on the identified Federal lands sampled[1]. Conversion from one wetland type to another occurred on Federal lands.

Urban expansion converted wetlands in various locations. Most notable occurrences were observed in the area around Hilton Head, Charleston and North Charleston and in the vicinity of Myrtle Beach and Columbia, South Carolina (Figure 24).

[1]Not all Federal ownership or boundaries are known.

Figure 22. An example of wetland loss to "other upland" land use in Horry County, South Carolina.

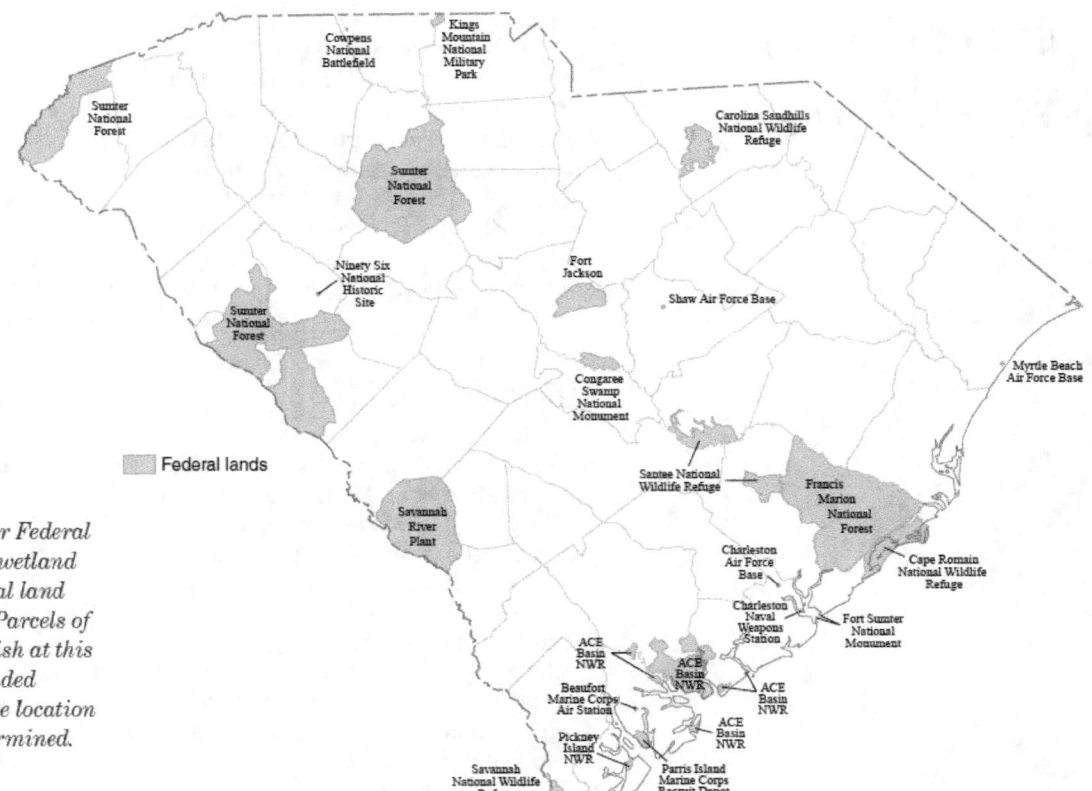

Figure 23. An illustration of major Federal land units in South Carolina. No wetland losses were observed within Federal land holdings between 1982 and 1989. Parcels of private land too small to distinguish at this scale were included within the shaded Federal ownship areas. The precise location of some Federal lands was undetermined.

Figure 24. Metropolitan (urban) lands in South Carolina (yellow). Losses of wetland to upland urban development were observed in those areas indicated in red.

■ Wetland loss 1983–1989

☐ Population centers

43

Discussion of Wetland Trends

Hefner *et al.* (1994) reported that wetland losses to upland in South Carolina were an estimated 6,100 acres (2,470 ha.) per year between 1972 and 1982. Findings from the present study indicate that this rate of loss has slowed. Based on data collected between 1982 and 1989, the annual wetland losses to upland were 2,920 acres (1,182 ha). This represents a 48 percent reduction in the annual rate of wetland loss.

Agriculture

From 1972 to 1982 agriculture was responsible for 41 percent of the wetland losses (Hefner *et al.* 1994). From 1982 to 1989 agriculture was responsible for 28 percent of the losses. This in combination with an overall reduction in the wetland loss rate for the State means that wetlands in agricultural areas have fared much better since the mid-1980s. This may have been related to agricultural programs that promote wetland conservation and disincentives for wetland drainage that have been in place since passage of the 1985 Food Security Act (Farm Bill).

During this study period, an estimated 2,520 acres (1,020 ha) of forested wetlands, 2,950 acres (1,194 ha) of palustrine shrub wetlands and 2,260 acres (915 ha) of palustrine emergent wetlands were lost to upland agriculture. Over 1,100 acres (445 ha) of vegetated wetlands were also converted to farmed wetlands.

Logging and Forestry

Although losses of wetlands due to agricultural activities have declined substantially, freshwater forested wetland area has been greatly reduced apparently resulting from silviculture and other logging and forestry practices[2]. Overall, forestry practices accounted for 31 percent of the total wetland losses between 1982 and 1989.

Freshwater forested wetlands declined by 125,000 acres (50,600 ha) between 1972 and 1982.

[2] This study did not differentiate between silvicultural operations and other clear cutting or logging operations involved in the removal of forest cover.

Thirty-three percent (4,170 acres or 1,690 ha.) of this area was converted to upland land uses (Hefner *et al.* 1994). From 1982 to 1989, forested wetlands diminished by 155,500 acres (62,960 ha.). While the loss of forested wetland to uplands either through drainage or filling, decreased from 4,170 acres (1,690 ha.) per year to an estimated 2,035 acres (824 ha.) per year, the amount of forested wetland area that changed increased from 12,500 acres (5,060 ha.) per year to 24,000 acres (9,714 ha.) per year. This is twice the area of wetland forests affected as compared to the previous study conducted by Hefner *et al.*(1994).

Of the forested wetlands lost to upland land uses, 40 percent or 5,340 acres (2,160 ha) were lost to upland-managed pine plantations. Another 2,480 acres (1,004 ha) were drained and converted to upland agriculture; 3,160 acres (1,280 ha) were lost to urban expansion and 1,520 acres (615 ha) were lost to rural development. Unidentified upland land uses were responsible for 720 acres (291 ha) of forested wetland losses. Similar trends have been reported for the Edisto River Basin where conversion of natural forest and agricultural land to planted loblolly pine has occurred at a very rapid rate (Marshall 1993).

Eighty-seven percent of the wetland forests where the trees were removed between 1982 and 1989 remained as another type of vegetated wetland. Seventy-five percent were re-classified as wetland shrubs and another 12 percent were wetland emergents. Figure 25 shows an area that had been wetland forest and is now re-classified as wetland emergents. An additional four percent (6,720 acres or 2,720 ha) were converted to lakes or ponds. Some of this conversion may have resulted from beaver impounding an area and drowning the trees. Other conversions result from man's activities by either creating new impoundments, holding ponds or by raising the water levels on existing impoundments and killing the trees (Tansey and Cost 1990).

Throughout the southeastern United States about 24 percent of the forest lands are owned or leased by the forest industry, largely for pulp and paper production and processing (McKnight *et al.* 1981). During the 1940s a technological innovation for processing young pine trees to make them suitable for newsprint had an effect on forestry operations throughout the southeastern United States. This development shifted pulpwood production from the northern states to the south and formed the basis for current forestry management practices. In 1980 pulpwood accounted for 75 percent of all the timber cut in South Carolina, the majority of it being pine trees (Kovacik and Winberry 1987).

Although bottomland hardwood and cypress trees produce valuable timber products, and continue to contribute substantially to the economy of the region (Langdon *et al.* 1981), they are fairly slow to regenerate and mature. The average rotation age of bottomland-cypress forests in the southern U.S. is about 65 years (Langdon *et al.* 1981). Conversely, pines replanted in the same areas and intensively managed with fertilizer and herbicide applications can attain a rotation age of 17 years in southern Georgia (Larry Mallard, Okefenokee National Wildlife Refuge, personal communication).

Maximum timber production with as short a harvest rotation as possible is the goal for commercial timber industries. For pulp and paper products industry this can best be achieved by the establishment of loblolly pine (*Pinus taeda*) plantations (Figure 26) in combination with silvicultural management actions (Malac *et al.* 1981; Allen and Campbell 1988). These intensive forest management techniques require the operation of heavy equipment during site preparation and planting, fertilizing and thinning operations, as well as during harvesting and slash disposal (Stenzel *et al.* 1985). This is a problem in many wetland forests in the southeast, since sites are accessible for only 3 to 6 months each year unless the area is drained of excess water. This has created a dilemma for the logging operations in the southeastern Coastal Plain where there are extensive wetland areas encountered on otherwise commercially valuable timberlands. The problem has been two-fold: 1) excess water limits operable season length and impedes the heavy equipment needed for forestry operations and 2) limited regeneration and productivity of pines planted on wet soils.

Figure 25. An area that had been a forested wetland one year prior to this photograph. The trees have been removed and the area is dominated by low shrubs and emergent plants. This represents a conversion from forested wetland to emergent wetland (Colleton County, South Carolina).

45

Initially, drainage practices alleviated excess water problems. Forested wetland drainage projects were initiated well before the 1950s and continued through the 1980s (as evidenced by this study) in attempts to drain soils sufficiently to increase yields on historically wet sites (Allen and Campbell 1988). Until very recently, normal silvicultural activities including earthmoving, planting, seeding, cultivating, minor drainage and harvesting were exempt from Federal regulation under Section 404 of the Clean Water Act (Welsch *et al*. 1995). In some cases drainage in combination with bedding was practiced to initiate seedling regeneration in wetlands. By the mid-1980s bedding sites was viewed as essential for the survival and rapid early growth of pine seedlings on poorly drained soils (Allen and Campbell 1988). These techniques were so successful from the

forestry standpoint that some pines exhibited height growth of 10 meters in only 12 years (Gent *et al*. 1986).

During the 1980s wetland drainage activities were being actively discouraged and some forestry operations shifted away from drainage practices and embarked on water management techniques to partially drain or manipulate water levels on wet soils to facilitate seedling survival and growth. The long-term impact(s) of such management actions on wetlands, especially on certain community types (*e.g.* pocosins and bays) has yet to be determined. Table 7 presents some current forest management and harvest actions that can effect wetlands in the southeastern United States.

By the late 1980s South Carolina had developed guidelines for wetland forest operations using "Best Management Practices" (Ice 1989; South Carolina Forestry Commission 1988). However, an analysis of voluntary compliance with the Best Management Practices in South Carolina indicated that where wetlands and poorly drained soils were predominant, problems with Best Management Practice implementation were apt to be more apparent (Hook *et al*. 1991).

Figure 26. Managed pine plantation of South Carolina's coastal plain. Intensively managed sites can obtain rapid harvest rotations for use by the pulp and paper industry.

Table 7. Potential timber and pulp production effects to wetlands.

Action	Effect
Road construction	Wetland loss; change hydrology, flow
Clearcutting	Changes habitat type/conditions; evapotranspiration differences
Fertilizers/herbicide application	Adds nutrients; reduces herbaceous competition; degrades runoff
Plantations	Changes species composition
Management of existing stands	Management for commercial value of forest products
Thinning	---------
Burning	Eliminates understory; adds nutrients
Bedding	Changes soil saturation; allows better growth of planted species (pines)
Patch cuttings	---------
Natural regeneration	May produce less desirable forest products; longer rotation cutting
Selective cutting	Targets commercially valuable species or stands
Drainage improvement	Wetland loss; change in hydrology
Water management	Changes hydrology; dewaters organic (peat) soils; organic soil oxidation
Levee construction	Wetland loss; changes periodicity of flooding; eliminates sediment/nutrient input
Channelization	Reduces or eliminates flooding

In 1995, the Environmental Protection Agency and the Army Corps of Engineers issued guidance at the Federal level describing Best Management Practices to protect water quality and hydrologic function when establishing pine plantations in wetlands. This guidance clarified the circumstances under which certain silvicultural activities are allowed in forested wetlands and outlines which mechanical silvicultural site preparation activities require a permit under the authority of the Clean Water Act (U.S. Environmental Protection Agency and Department of the Army 1995).

Whatever the reasons, the data on forested wetlands collected as part of this study indicate that in South Carolina, forested wetlands are disappearing at the rate of 5.4 percent per year as these areas are converted to upland land uses and other types of wetlands. Logging, forestry practices and forest management may influence South Carolina's wetlands into the future.

Urban and Rural Development

Urbanization and rural development contributed substantially to losses of wetlands in certain areas of the State between 1982 and 1989. The demands for land for building will potentially have an affect on South Carolina's wetland resources if this trend continues. Key areas include the Hilton Head area of Beaufort County; the Charleston and North Charleston metropolitan complex; the Myrtle Beach areas of Horry County and the high growth communities of the Rolling Plain. Figure 27 shows the

counties in South Carolina exhibiting high population growth through 1990. It is anticipated that conflicts between land development interests and wetlands will persist in these areas. By using this demographic information in combination with the results obtained during this study it is possible to illustrate which wetlands may be most vulnerable to development pressure in the future (Figure 28).

Urban development was the second leading cause for the loss of forested wetlands to upland between 1982 and 1989 (24 percent). When urban development and rural development are combined they account for 35 percent of the palustrine forested wetlands lost to uplands during this study. Activities that convert wetlands to the upland urban and upland rural development categories should be regulated actions and fall under Federal and/or State jurisdiction.

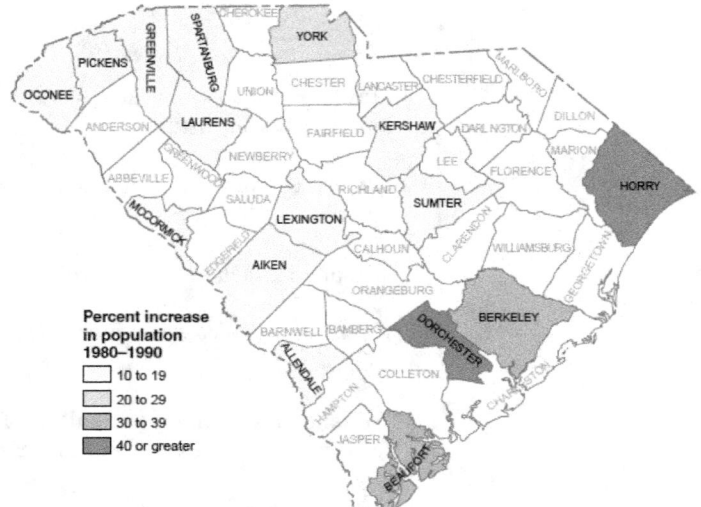

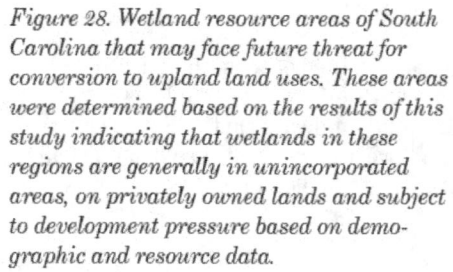

Figure 27. Population growth in South Carolina counties between 1980 and 1990 (Source: U.S. Bureau of Census 1992).

Figure 28. Wetland resource areas of South Carolina that may face future threat for conversion to upland land uses. These areas were determined based on the results of this study indicating that wetlands in these regions are generally in unincorporated areas, on privately owned lands and subject to development pressure based on demographic and resource data.

Summary

South Carolina had an estimated 4,104,850 acres (1,661,880 ha) of wetlands in 1989. The average annual net loss of wetlands was 2,920 acres (1,182 ha) and total wetland area declined by 0.5 percent from 1982 and 1989.

The rate of wetland loss in South Carolina declined by 48 percent compared to the previous study period. This was probably due to a decline in the number of wetland acres converted to agriculture following passage of legislation to discourage wetland conversion in the mid-1980s. Other wetland conservation measures within the State undoubtedly contributed to this declining loss rate.

When all losses and gains of wetlands were tallied, South Carolina has not attained no-net-loss of wetland area within the time frame of this study.

Loss of palustrine forested wetlands continue to contribute substantially to the loss of wetland area. To date, improved forest management practices in combination with farm land abandonment and shifts away from commodity crops such as cotton and tobacco to growing trees are helping sustain South Carolina's forested resources. Future monitoring will be necessary to determine the effectiveness of new guidance for the Best Management Practices of forested wetlands.

Urban expansion and development in the rapidly growing areas of the Coastal Flats and Gulf-Atlantic Rolling Plain may put pressure on all natural resources in those parts of the State. In future years there will be an increasing challenge to balance population and economic growth with wetland protection.

Cooper River, South Carolina
M. Caldwell

References Cited

Allen, H.L. and R.G. Campbell. 1988. Wet site pine management in the Southeastern United States. *In:* D.D. Hook, W.H. McKee, Jr., H.K. Smith, J. Gregory, V.G. Burrell, Jr., M.R. DeVoe, R.E. Sojka, S. Gilbert, R. Banks, L.H. Stolzy, C. Brooks, T.D. Matthews, and T.H. Shear (eds.). The ecology and management of wetlands. Vol 2. Timber Press, Portland, OR. pp.173–184.

Anderson, J.R., E.E. Hardy, J.T. Roach and R.E. Winter. 1976. A land use and land cover classification system for use with remote sensor data. U.S. Geological Survey Professional Paper 964. U.S. Geological Survey, Washington, D.C. 28 p.

Aulbach-Smith, C.A. and S.J. de Kozlowski. 1990. Aquatic and Wetlands Plants of South Carolina. South Carolina Aquatic Plant Management Council in cooperation with S.C. Water Resources Comm. 123 p.

Bailey, R.G. 1980. Description of the Ecoregions of the United States. USDA-Forest Service. Misc. Publication No. 1391. 77 pp.

Barry, J.M. 1980. National Vegetation of South Carolina. Univ. of South Carolina Press, Columbia, SC. 214 p.

Beasley, B.R. D.A. Lange, K.T. Newland and W.C. Brittain. 1988. South Carolina Rivers Assessment. Report No. 164. South Carolina Water Resources Commission, Columbia, SC. 249 p.

Beauchamp, K.H. 1987. A history of drainage and drainage methods. *In:* Pavelis, G.A. (ed.), Farm drainage in the United States — history, status and prospects. Washington, D.C., Economic Research Service, U.S. Department of Agriculture, Miscellaneous Publication No 1455, pp. 13–29.

Bebber, T.L. 1988. South Carolina Wetlands Study A Component of the State Comprehensive Outdoor Recreation Plan. South Carolina Dept. of Parks, Recreation, and Tourism, Division of Engineering and Planning. Columbia, SC. 235 p.

Brunswig, N. and K. Lake. 1991. Wildlife Sanctuaries, National Audubon Society Sanctuary Dept. Sharon, CT. 42 p.

Clark, J.R. and J. Benforado. 1981. Wetlands of Bottonland hardwood forests. Elsevier Scientific Publishing CO. Amsterdam. 401 p.

Colquhoun, D.J. 1974. Cyclic surficial stratigraphic units of the middle and lower coastal plains, central South Carolina. *In:* Oaks, R.Q. DuBar, J.R. (eds.), Postmiocene Stratigraphy Central and Southern Atlantic Coastal Plain, Utah Sate Univ. Press. pp. 179–190.

Cowardin, L.M, V. Carter, F.C. Golet, and E.T. LaRoe. 1979. Classification of wetlands and deepwater habitats of the United States. U.S. Fish and Wildlife Service, Washington, D.C. 131 p.

Dahl, T.E. 1990. Wetland losses in the United States 1780's to 1980's. U.S. Department of the Interior, Fish and Wildlife Service, Washington, D.C. 13 pp.

Dahl, T.E. and C. Johnson. 1991. Status and trends of wetlands in the conterminous United States, mid 1970's to mid 1980's. U.S. Department of the Interior, Fish and Wildlife Service, Washington, D.C. 28 p.

De Francesco, D.J. 1988. Orangeburg County Soil Survey. U.S. Department of Agriculture, SoilConservation Service, Washington, D.C.

Durham, E. 1967. Woody Plants of the Congaree Forest Swamp, South Carolina. Ecological Studies leaflet No. 12. The Nature Conservancy. 5 p.

Ewel, K.C. and H.T. Odum (eds). 1984. Cypress Swamps. University of Florida Press, Gainesville, FL 472 p.

Ferguson, R.L., L.L. Wood and D.B. Graham. 1993. Monitoring spatial change in seagrass habitat with aerial photography. Photogrammetric Engineering and Remote Sensing, 59(6): 1033–1038.

Garrett, W.E. (ed.). 1988. Historical atlas of the United Sates. National Geographic Society, Washington, D.C. 289 p.

Gent, J.A., Jr., H.L. Allen, R.G. Campbell, and C.G. Wells. 1986. Magnitude, duration and economic analysis of loblolly pine growth response following bedding and phosphorus fertilization, Southern Journal of Applied Foresty 10: 124–128.

Gibson, G. (ed.). 1994. South Carolina Statistical Abstract 1994. Office of Research and Statistical Services, South Carolina State Budget and Control Board. Columbia, SC. 430 p.

Hammond, E.H. 1970. Physical subdivisions of the United States of America. *In:* U.S. Geological Survey. National atlas of the United States of America. Department of the Interior, Washington, D.C. 61 p.

Hefner, J.M., B.O. Wilen, T.E. Dahl and W.E. Frayer. 1994. Southeast wetlands; status and trends, mid-1970's to mid-1980's. U.S. Department of the Interior, Fish and Wildlife Service, Atlanta, GA. 32 p.

Hook, D., W. McKee, T. Williams, B. Baker, L. Lundquist, R. Martin and J. Mills. 1991. A survey of voluntary compliance of forestry best management practices in South Carolina during the period 1988-1990. South Carolina Forestry Commission. 23 p. plus appendix.

Ice. G.G. 1989. The effectiveness of silvicultural nonpoint source control programs for several southern states. In: D.D. Hook and R. Lea (eds.) Proceedings of the symposium: The forested wetlands of the southern United States. Gen. Tech. Rept. SE-50. U.S. Department of Agriculture, Forest Service, Asheville, NC. pp. 163–168.

Jones, R.H. 1981. A classification of lowland forests in the northern coastal plain of South Carolina. M.S. Thesis. Clemson University, Clemson, SC. 177 p.

Kane, S. and R. Keeton. 1993. Southern National Forests. FalconPress Publishing Co., Inc. Helena, MT in cooperation with the Forest Service, U.S. Department of Agriculture. 159 p.

Kovacik, C.F. and J.J. Winberry. 1987. South Carolina A Geography. Westview Press, Boulder, CO. 235 p.

Laderman, A.D. 1982. Comparative community structure of Charmaecyparis thyoides bog forests: Canapoy diversity. Wetlands, Vol. 2. pp. 216–230.

Laderman, A.D. 1989. The ecology of the Atlantic white cedar: A community profile. U.S. Fish and Wildlife Service Biol. Rept. 85 (7.21). 114 p.

Langbein, W.B, and K.T. Iseri. 1960. General introduction and hydrologic definitions manual of hydrology. Part 1. General surface water techniques. U.S. Geologocal Survey, Water Supply Paper 1541-A. 29 p.

Langdon, O.G., J.P. McClure, D.D. Hook, J.M. Crockett and R. Hunt. 1981. Extent, condition, management, and research needs of bottomland hardwood — cypress forests in the Southeastern United States. In: J.R. Clark and J. Benforado (eds.). Wetlands of bottomland hardwood forests. Elsevier Scientific Pub. Co. Amsterdam. pp. 71–85.

Lide, R.F., V.G. Meentemeyer, J.E. Pinder, III. and L.M. Beatty. 1995. Hydrology of a Carolina Bay located on the upper Coastal Plain of Western South Carolina. Wetlands, Vol. 15, No. 1. pp 47–57.

Littlefield, D.C. 1995. Rice and the making of South Carolina. S.C. Department of Archives and History. Columbia, SC. 38 p.

Lucas, S.E., Jr. 1980. Mills Atlas of the State of South Carolina 1825. Southern Historical Press, Inc. Greenville, SC. 43 p. plus maps.

Marshall, W.D. 1993. Assessing change in the Edisto River Basin: An ecological characterization. South Carolina Water Resources Commission, Report No. 177. Columbia, SC. 149 p.

Meador, M.R. 1996. South Carolina Wetland Resources. In: J.D. Fretwell, J.S. Williams and P.J. Redman (eds.). National Water Summary on Wetlands Resources. U.S. Geological Survey, Water Supply Paper 2425, Reston, VA. pp. 345–349.

Menzel, R.G. and C. M. Cooper. 1992. Small impoundments and ponds. In: C.T. Hackney, S.M. Adams and W.H. Martin (eds.). Biodiversity of the southeastern United States-aquatic communities. John Wiley and Sons, Inc., NY. pp. 389–420.

McKnight, J.S., D.D. Hook, O.G. Langdon and R.L. Johnson. 1981. Flood tolerance and related characteristics of trees of the bottonland forests of the southern United States. In: J.R. Clark and J. Benforado (eds). Wetlands of bottonland hardwood forests. Elsevier Scientific Pub. Co. Amsterdam. pp. 29–69.

Nelson, J.B. 1986. The Natural Communities of South Carolina. South Carolina Wildlife and Marine Resources Dept. 55 p.

Orth, R.J., K.A. Moore and J.F. Nowak. 1990. Monitoring Seagrass distribution and abundance patterns: A case study from the Chesapeake Bay. In: S.J. Kiraly, F.A. Cross and J.D. Buffington (eds.). Federal coastal wetland mapping programs. Biol. Rept. 90 (18). Fish and Wildlife Service, Washington, D.C. pp. 111–123.

Powell, D.S., J.L. Faulkner, D.R. Darr, Z. Zhu and D.W. CacCleery. 1993. Forest resources of the United States, 1992. U.S. Department of Agriculture, Forest Service. General Technical Report RM-234, Washington, D.C. 132 p.

Reed, P.B. 1988. National list of plant species that occur in wetlands: South Carolina. NERC-88/18.40. U.S. Fish and Wildlife Service, Washington, D.C.

Richardson, C.J. and J. W. Gibbons. 1993. Pocosins, Carolina Bays and Montain Bogs. In: W.H. Martin, S.G. Boyce and A.C. Echternacht (eds.). Biodiversity of the southeastern United States-lowland terrestrial communities. John Wily and Sons, Inc. New York. pp. 257–310.

Salley, A.S. Jr. 1919. The introduction of Rice Culture into South Carolina. Bulletins of the Historical Commission of South Carolina No. 6. Columbia, SC. 23 p.

Sharitz, R. R. and J.W. Gibbons. 1982. The ecology of southwestern shrub boys (pocosins) and Carolina bays: a community profile. U.S. Fish and Wildlife Service, Washington, D.C. FWS/OBS - 82/04. 93 p.

South Carolina Coastal Council. 1982. Understanding our coastal environment. Charleston, SC. 40 p.

South Carolina Forestry Commission. 1988. Best management practices for South Carolina's Forest Wetlands. 20 p.

South Carolina State Budget and Control Board. 1984. South Carolina statistical abstract. Office of Research and Statistical Services, Columbia, SC. 430 p.

Stenzel, G., T.A. Walbridge, Jr. and J.K. Pearce. 1985. Logging and pulpwood production. John Wiley and Sons, Inc. NY. 358 p.

Tansey, J. B. and N. D. Cost. 1990. Estimating the forest-wetland resource in the southeastern United States with forest survey data. In: B.D. Jackson (ed). Forest Ecology and Management Vol. 33/34, Nos. 1-4. pp. 193–213.

Taylor, J.R., M.A. Cardamore and W.J. Mitsch. 1990. Bottomland Hardwood forests: their functions and values. In: J.G. Gosselink, L.C. Lee and T.A. Muir (eds). Ecological Processes and Cumulative Impacts: Illustrated by Bottomland

Hardwood Wetland Ecosystems. Lewis Publishers, Inc. Chelsea, MI. pp. 13–86.

U.S. Bureau of the Census. 1992. USA counties: A statistical abstract supplement on CD-ROM. U.S. Department of Commerce, Washington, D.C.

U.S. Department of Agriculture. 1975 Soil taxonomy: A basic system of soil classification for making and interpreting soil surveys. Soil Conservation Service, Soil Survey Staff, Agricultural Handbook 436, Washington, D.C. 754 p.

U.S. Department of Agriculture. 1991. Hydric Soils of the United States. Soil Conservation Service, Miscellaneous Publication Number 1491, Washington, D.C.

U.S. Environmental Protection Agency and U. S. Department of the Army. 1995. Memorandum to the field — Application of best management practices to mechanical silvicultural site preparation activities for the establishment of pine plantations in the southeast. Washington, D.C. 8 p.

U.S. Fish and Wildlife Service. 1994a. Continuous Wetlands Trend Analysis Project Specifications (Photointerpretation and Cartographic Procedures). Wetland Status and Trends, National Wetlands Inventory Center, St. Petersburg, FL. 60 p.

U.S. Fish and Wildlife Service. 1994b. Mapping Report for United States Air Force: Shaw Air Force Base. Open File Report, National Wetlands Inventory Center, St. Petersburg, FL.

U.S. Fish and Wildlife Service. 1994c. Mapping Report for United States Navy: Naval Weapons Station, Charleston, SC. Open File Report, National Wetlands Inventory Center, St. Petersburg, FL.

U.S. Fish and Wildlife Service. 1995. Photointerpretation Conventions of the National Wetlands Inventory, National Wetlands Inventory Center, St. Petersburg, FL. 60 p.

U.S. Geological Survey. 1970. The national atlas of the United States of America. U.S. Department of the Interior, Washington, D.C. 417 p.

Wells, J.T. and C.H. Peterson. Date Unknown. Atlantic and Gulf Coastal Barriers. LA Sea Grant College Program, LA State Univ., Baton Rouge, LA. 15 p.

Welsch, D.J., D.L. Smart, J.N. Boyer, P. Minkin, H.C. Smith and T. L. McCandless. 1995. Forested wetlands: Functions, benifits and the use of best management practices. U.S. Department of Agriculture, Forest Service. NA-PR-01-95, Radnor, PA. 63 p.

Wharton, C.H., W.M. Kitchens, E.C. Pendleton, and T.W. Sipe. 1982. The ecology of bottomland hardwood swamps of the Southwest: a community profile. U.S. Fish and Wildlife Service, Washington, D.C. FWS/OBS–81/37. 133 p.

Wharton, C.H., V.W. Lambou, J. Newsom, P.V. Winger, L.L. Gaddy and R. Manake. 1981. The fauna of bottomland hardwoods in the Southeastern United States. In: J.R. Clark and J. Benforado (eds.). Wetlands of bottomland hardwood forests. Elsevier Scientific Pub. Co. Amsterdam. pp. 87–160.

Williams, M. 1989. Americans and Their Forests A Historical Geography. Cambridge University Press. 599 p.

Winton, C.G. 1980. Breeding bird census: virgin hardwood swamp forest. Amer. Birds 34(1): 41–44; 50.

Appendix A

DEFINITIONS OF HABITAT CATEGORIES USED IN THE SOUTH CAROLINA STATUS AND TRENDS STUDY

WETLANDS[1]:

In general terms, wetlands are lands where saturation with water is the dominate factor determining the nature of soil development and the types of plant and animal communities living in the soil and on its surface. The single feature that most wetlands share is soil or substrate that is at least periodically saturated with or covered by water. The water creates severe physiological problems for all plants and animals except those that are adapted for life in water or in saturated soil.

Wetlands are lands transitional between terrestrial and aquatic systems where the water table is usually at or near the surface or the land is covered by shallow water. For purposes of this classification wetlands must have one or more of the following three attributes: (1) at least periodically, the land supports predominantly hydrophytes,[2] (2) the substrate is predominantly undrained hydric soil,[3] and (3) the substrate is nonsoil and is saturated with water or covered by shallow water at some time during the growing season of each year.

The term wetland includes a variety of areas that fall into one of five categories: (1) areas with hydrophytes and hydric soils, such as those commonly known as marshes, swamps, and bogs; (2) areas without hydrophytes but with hydric soils—for example, flats where drastic fluctuation in water level, wave action, turbidity, or high concentration of salts may prevent the growth of hydrophytes; (3) areas with hydrophytes but nonhydric soils, such as margins of impoundments or excavations where hydrophytes have become established but hydric soils have not yet developed; (4) areas without soils but with hydrophytes such as the seaweed-covered portions of rocky shores; and (5) wetlands without soil and without hydrophytes, such as gravel beaches or rocky shores without vegetation.

Marine System

The Marine System consists of the open ocean overlying the continental shelf and its associated high-energy coastline. Marine habitats are exposed to the waves and currents of the open ocean and the water regimes are determined primarily by the ebb and flow of oceanic tides. Salinities exceed 30 parts per thousand, with little or no dilution except outside the mouths of estuaries. Shallow coastal indentations or bays without appreciable freshwater inflow, and coasts with exposed rocky islands that provide the mainland with little or no shelter from wind and waves, are also considered part of the Marine System because they generally support typical marine biota.

Estuarine System

The Estuarine System consists of deepwater tidal habitats and adjacent tidal wetlands that are usually semi-enclosed by land but have open, partly obstructed, or sporadic access to the open ocean, and in which ocean water is at least occasionally diluted by freshwater runoff from the land. The salinity may be periodically increased above that of the open ocean by evaporation. Along some low-energy coastlines there is appreciable dilution of sea water. Offshore areas with typical estuarine plants and animals, such as red mangroves (Rhizophora mangle) and eastern oysters (Crassostrea virginica), are also included in the Estuarine System.

---

1 Adapted from Cowardin et al. 1979.
2 The U.S. Fish and Wildlife Service has published the list of plant species that occur in wetlands of the United States (Reed 1988).
3 U.S. Department of Agriculture has developed the list of hydric soils for the United States (U.S. Department of Agriculture 1991).

Marine and Estuarine Subsystems

Subtidal   The substrate is continuously submerged by marine or estuarine waters.

Intertidal   The substrate is exposed and flooded by tides. Intertidal includes the splash zone of coastal waters.

Palustrine   SystemThe Palustrine System includes all nontidal wetlands dominated by trees, shrubs, persistent emergents, emergent mosses or lichens, farmed wetlands, and all such wetlands that occur in tidal areas where salinity due to ocean derived salts is below 0.5 parts per thousand. It also includes wetlands lacking such vegetation, but with all of the following four characteristics:
(1) area less than 8 Ha (20 acres); (2) active wave formed or bedrock shoreline features lacking; (3) water depth in the deepest part of basin less than 2 meters at low water; and (4) salinity due to ocean derived salts less than 0.5 parts per thousand.

Classes

Unconsolidated
Bottom   Unconsolidated Bottom includes all wetlands with at least 25 percent cover of particles smaller than stones, and a vegetative cover less than 30 percent. Examples of unconsolidated substrates are: sand, mud, organic material, cobble-gravel.

Aquatic Bed   Aquatic Beds are dominated by plants that grow principally on or below the surface of the water for most of the growing season in most years. Examples include: seagrass beds[4], pondweeds (Pontamogeton spp.), wild celery (Vallisneria americana), waterweed (Elodea spp.), and duckweed (Lemna spp.).

Rocky Shore   Rocky Shore includes wetland environments characterized by bedrock, stones, or boulders which singly or in combination have an areal cover of 75 percent or more and an areal vegetative coverage of less than 30 percent.

Unconsolidated
Shore   Unconsolidated Shore includes all wetland habitats having two characteristics: (1) unconsolidated substrates with less than 75 percent areal cover of stones, boulders or bedrock and; (2) less than 30 percent areal cover of vegetation other than pioneering plants.

Emergent
Wetland   Emergent Wetlands are characterized by erect, rooted, herbaceous hydrophytes, excluding mosses and lichens. This vegetation is present for most of the growing season in most years. These wetlands are usually dominated by perennial plants.

Shrub Wetland   Shrub Wetlands include areas dominated by woody vegetation less than 6 meters (20 feet) tall. The species include true shrubs, young trees, and trees or shrubs that are small or stunted because of environmental conditions.

---

[4] Although some seagrass beds may be evident on aerial photography, water and climatic conditions often prevent their detection.

Forested Wetland	Forested Wetlands are characterized by woody vegetation that is 6 meters tall or taller.
Farmed Wetland	Farmed wetlands are wetlands that meet the Cowardin et al. definition where the soil surface has been mechanically or physically altered for production of crops, but hydrophytes will become re-established if farming is discontinued.

DEEPWATER HABITATS:

Wetlands and deepwater habitats are defined separately because the term wetland has not included deep permanent water bodies. For the purposes of conducting status and trends studies, Riverine and Lacustrine are considered deepwater habitats. Elements of Marine or Estuarine systems can be wetland or deepwater. Palustrine includes only wetland habitats.

Deepwater Habitats are permanently flooded land lying below the deepwater of wetlands. Deepwater habitats include environments where surface water is permanent and often deep, so that water, rather than air, is the principal medium within which the dominant organisms live, whether or not they are attached to the substrate. As in wetlands, the dominant plants are hydrophytes; however, the substrates are considered nonsoil because the water is too deep to support emergent vegetation (U.S. Department of Agriculture 1975).

Riverine System	The Riverine System includes deepwater habitats contained within a channel, with the exception of habitats with water containing ocean derived salts in excess of 0.5 parts per thousand. A channel is "an open conduit either naturally or artificially created which periodically or continuously contains moving water, or which forms a connecting link between two bodies of standing water" (Langbein and Iseri 1960).
Lacustrine System	The Lacustrine System includes deepwater habitats with all of the following characteristics: (1) situated in a topographic depression or a dammed river channel; (2) lacking trees, shrubs, persistent emergents, emergent mosses or lichens with greater than 30 percent coverage; (3) total area exceeds 8 ha (20 acres). Similar wetland and deepwater habitats totaling less than 8 ha are also included in the Lacustrine System if an active, wave-formed or bedrock shoreline feature makes up all or part of the boundary, or if the water depth in the deepest part of the basin exceeds 2 m (6.6 feet) at low water.

UPLANDS:

Agriculture[5]	Agricultural land may be defined broadly as land used primarily for production of food and fiber. Agricultural activity is evidenced by distinctive geometric field and road patterns on the landscape and the traces produced by livestock or mechanized equipment. Examples of agricultural land use include: cropland and pasture, orchards, groves, vineyards, nurseries, cultivated lands, and ornamental horticultural areas including sod farms, confined feeding operations, and other agricultural land including livestock feed lots, farmsteads including houses, support structures (silos) and adjacent yards, barns, poultry sheds, etc.

---

[5] Adapted from Anderson et al. 1976.

Urban

Urban land is comprised of areas of intensive use with much of the land covered by structures (high building density). Urbanized areas are cities and towns that provide the goods and services needed to survive by modern day standards through a Central Business District. Services such as banking, medical and legal office buildings, supermarkets and department stores make up the business center of a city. Commercial strip developments along main transportation routes, shopping centers, contiguous dense residential areas, industrial and commercial complexes, transportation, power and communication facilities, city parks, ball fields and golf courses can also be included in the urban category.

Forested
Plantation

Forested plantations include areas of planted and managed forest stands such as those in the Southeastern United States. Planted pines, Christmas tree farms, clear cuts and other managed forest stands, such as Hardwood Forestry, will be included in this category.

Rural
Development

Rural developments occur in sparse rural and suburban settings outside distinct urban cities and towns. These communities depend on urban areas for the goods and services found in a Central Business District. They are characterized by non-intensive land use and sparse building density. Typically, a rural development is a cross-roads community with a corner gas station and convenience store surrounded by sparse residential housing and agriculture. Scattered suburban communities located outside a major urban center can also be included in this category as well as some industrial and commercial complexes, isolated transportation, power and communication facilities, strip mines, quarries, and recreational areas such as golf courses, etc. Major highways through rural development areas are included the rural development category.

Other Land Use

Other Land Use is composed of uplands not characterized by the previous categories. Typically these lands would include native prairie; unmanaged or non-patterned upland forests and scrub lands; and barren land. Lands in transition may also fit into this category.

Appendix B

This table presents acreage, in thousands of acres, and the estimated number of acres that changed classification between 1982 and 1989. The columns (across) identify the 1982 classification with the column labeled "Time 1" containing the acreage totals for that year. The rows (down) identify the classification and acreage for 1989. The row labeled "Time 2" contains the totals for 1989. The number under the acreage estimate for each entry is the percent coefficient of variation for that estimate.

(In each cell the first number is the acreage estimate; the number in parentheses is the percent coefficient of variation. A "." indicates a missing entry.)

WETLAND TYPE	M2	E1UB	E2EM	E2SS	E2US	RIV	PFO	PSS	PEM	PUS	PUB	PAB	Pf	LAC	M1	AGRIC	URBAN	UFP	URD	OTHER	TIME1	WETLAND TYPE
M2	1442(38)	0	9(88)	0	0	0	0	0	0	0	0	0	0	0	793(83)	0	0	0	0	0	2244(38)	M2
E1UB	47(71)	348539(10)	301(35)	0	820(38)	0	.	.	0	0	.	0	0	.	0	0	0	0	0	0	349706(10)	E1UB
E2EM	367(74)	104(56)	410688(9)	317(50)	200(50)	0	0	5(87)	2(87)	0	13(87)	5(87)	0	11(87)	47(87)	4(87)	0	0	0	0	411762(9)	E2EM
E2SS	0	18(52)	84(88)	3424(23)	0	0	0	0	0	0	4(87)	0	0	0	0	0	0	0	0	0	3530(23)	E2SS
E2US	2(87)	535(41)	161(39)	30(87)	25218(22)	0	.	0	0	0	0	0	0	0	.	0	0	0	0	72(50)	26018(21)	E2US
RIV	.	0	0	0	0	70208(18)	.	15(96)	36(96)	0	0	0	.	743(96)	0	0	0	0	0	0	71002(18)	RIV
PFO	0	0	0	0	0	0	2803697	195754(11)	18913(26)	76(66)	3600(16)	429(69)	122(51)	2646(52)	0	2520(34)	3163(41)	5342(42)	1520(76)	766(51)	3038551(5)	PFO
PSS	4(87)	.	0	0	0	0	78906(21)	283811(15)	14915(50)	0	1515(31)	41(96)	275(60)	367(65)	0	2949(55)	572(40)	1333(81)	117(40)	60(47)	384864(14)	PSS
PEM	0	0	0	0	0	0	339(49)	32975(21)	129356(15)	20(76)	1779(21)	15(72)	1054(42)	813(60)	0	2257(29)	297(35)	123(65)	246(56)	335(47)	169610(13)	PEM
PUS	.	0	0	0	0	.	0	25(79)	66(57)	624(42)	392(68)	5(96)	0	0	0	0	0	0	0	0	1113(34)	PUS
PUB	0	0	0	0	0	0	31(95)	258(37)	2627(18)	189(55)	68186(7)	519(45)	0	25(79)	0	143(58)	153(71)	0	66(69)	178(94)	72377(6)	PUB
PAB	.	.	0	0	0	0	0	26(95)	20(96)	0	158(84)	1167(28)	0	0	0	5(95)	0	0	0	0	1376(26)	PAB
Pf	0	0	0	0	0	.	10(96)	239(43)	87(50)	0	15(96)	0	11888(23)	0	0	66(52)	0	0	0	0	12305(23)	Pf
LAC	0	0	0	0	0	.	0	.	644(56)	177(88)	0	0	0	220068(27)	0	0	0	0	0	0	220890(27)	LAC
M1	242(87)	0	0	0	0	0	0	0	0	0	0	0	0	0	109969(31)	0	0	0	0	0	110211(31)	M1
AGRIC	.	.	.	.	.	.	.	.	.	.	.	.	.	.	.	.	.	.	.	.	.	AGRIC
URBAN	.	.	.	.	.	.	.	.	.	.	.	.	.	.	.	.	.	.	.	.	.	URBAN
UFP	.	.	.	.	.	.	.	.	.	.	.	.	.	.	.	.	.	.	.	.	.	UFP
URD	.	.	.	.	.	.	.	.	.	.	.	.	.	.	.	.	.	.	.	.	.	URD
OTHER	.	2(87)	0	0	86(67)	25(96)	41(95)	61(72)	66(44)	87(69)	2146(13)	0	0	6064(72)	0	.	.	.	.	.	.	OTHER
TIME2	2103(35)	349197(10)	411246(9)	3771(22)	26324(21)	70234(18)	2883066(5)	513283(10)	167395(13)	1225(29)	80825(6)	2182(2)	13430(22)	236272(26)	110808(31)	.	.	.	.	.	.	TIME2

Appendix C

This table presents the acreage estimates (first line) and the percent coefficient of variation (second line) for the acreage change occurring in combined wetland and deepwater categories between 1982 and 1989. Estuarine totals represent the estuarine wetland types including estuarine emergents, shrubs and unconsolidated shores. Deepwater totals include all lacustrine and riverine acreage estimates. Palustrine totals include the freshwater wetland types including palustrine forest, shrub, emergent, unconsolidated shore, unconsolidated bottom and aquatic bed.

WETLAND TYPE	Estuarine	Deepwater	Palustrine	Marine	Agriculture	Urban	Forested Plantation	Rural Development	Other Upland	TIME1	WETLAND TYPE
Estuarine	441942	668	29	839	4	0	0	0	72	443553	Estuarine
	9	38	72	83	87	.	.	.	50	9	
Deepwater	1167	639559	872	0	0	0	0	0	0	641598	Deepwater
	33	11	45	.	.	.	.	.	.	11	
Palustrine	4	3851	3654127	.	7940	4186	6799	1950	1339	3680196	Palustrine
	87	44	5	.	27	32	41	61	39	4	
Marine	242	0	0	109969	0	0	0	0	0	110211	Marine
	87	.	.	31	.	.	.	.	.	31	
Agriculture	4	2536	2734	0							Agriculture
	87	52	17	.							
Urban	0	0	73	0							Urban
	.	.	38	.							
Forested Plantation	0	2994	909	0							Forested Plantation
	.	90	19	.							
Rural Development	0	5	262	0							Rural Development
	.	96	52	.							
Other Upland	86	6091	2401	0							Other Upland
	67	72	13	.							
TIME2	443444	655703	3661406	110808							TIME2
	9	11	5	31							

U.S. Department of the Interior
U. S. Fish & Wildlife Service

http://www.fws.gov

December 1999

www.ingramcontent.com/pod-product-compliance
Lightning Source LLC
Chambersburg PA
CBHW081116280526
45787CB00007B/2861